FINDING AND FINANCING APARTMENT BUILDINGS

Proven ways to get it done

Alex Oliver
Emily Oliver

Dedication:

Thank you to our family and friends who helped make this book possible.

And to all the people who help our dream of real-estate investing come true.

Our Background

You can trust us and the information we are about to share because we have been successful apartment investors for more than 10 years. We started with just a desire to invest. Then, through seminars, classes, talking to people, and hard knocks, we learned how to invest in apartments successfully. Since we managed our own properties from the beginning, we now know the ins and outs of how to acquire them, how to manage them, and how to run them. We are excited to share what we have learned with you.

Hi everyone and welcome to your apartment investing roadmap. We are Emily and Alex Oliver, your apartment investing experts here to discuss the steps that every apartment investor needs to follow to get the best results and succeed with apartment investing. Welcome!

We will start with a little bit about our background and experience, so you can understand who we are, where we come from, and how we can relate to where you are right now.

Actually, neither of us have a background in real estate or business. We both went to school to study Mechanical Engineering. Alex focused on robotics and loved the logic that robots follow. Whatever the input, there is always a guaranteed output. There is a term that we used while in school, garbage in – garbage out. This logical thinking has helped both of us with real estate deals. Alex was very close to staying in school for many more years to focus on robotics and become a professor.

However, instead, Alex decided that he was ready to enter the working world and took a corporate job after graduation.

The job Alex took out of college was part of a leadership development program that moved us around the country. Every year or so, we would move to a different city and work on various projects. Some of the projects saved his company millions of dollars, but we never saw any of that money. That was when we realized that very few people get rich working for large companies. Then in 2006 the company Alex worked for moved us to St. Louis, Missouri, and that's when we started our real estate career.

Some might think that this was a terrible time to start investing. No one remembers the 2008 crash more than us, but we found that having experience in so many different market conditions has helped us better understand the basic principles of apartment investing and be able to share these lessons with you.

A lot of people wonder if we have taken any formal training relating to apartment investing. The answer is yes, and no. Like many real estate investors, especially when you're coming from a corporate world, we went to a lot of investment seminars on various subjects including probate, flipping, stock investing, starting a business, and wholesaling, just to name a few. After sorting through all the information, we found the niche of apartment investing made the most sense for us. It really is a business to manage. Then Alex went to the St. Louis Apartment Association to become a certified apartment manager and enhance his skills. Overall, we have learned a lot on the job, but also try to incorporate any education that is available in order to enhance our knowledge.

To let you know where we started, as beginning apartment investors in early 2009, Alex had to call 27 banks before we found one that would finance our first building. This was when the market was down, and banks were very hesitant to do any apartment financing. We did finally get the funding, and, within nine months, we were able to get back all the initial cash plus some extra.

Now after years of experience, many successful projects and a lot of learning and hard work, we are ready to share what we know to help you find your success in apartment investing.

SECTION 1:

FOUNDATIONS FOR SUCCESS

The Most Important Steps for Success

The first and most important step in apartment investing is to understand yourself, your finances, and your goals before you even consider looking at a property. Your success and all the money you will ever make on a deal is predetermined on the day you buy. Therefore, it is critical that you start by taking the time to understand what you want and where you are going. The best way for you to take this step is to complete a self-assessment.

Understand Yourself and What You Want

This is a time to be as objective as possible.

How much time do you want to spend on this investment? Do you want to be a hands-on property manager or hands-off investor? If you are thinking hands-on, are you willing to give up every night and weekend (if you are currently working a full-time job)? Will you give up family time? Are you willing to be on site every day, once a week, once a month or does never sound better? Maybe you would prefer to be more of an investor and have somebody else take care of it. Any of these are alright. It is just determining what is best for you.

You might start by tracking where you currently spend your time to determine how much time you are willing to commit to a new project. Below is an example of a time tracker that we have used for this purpose. Ours was in

Time	Task
6:00 AM	Wake Up
6:15 AM	Check email
6:30 AM	Check email
6:45 AM	Shower
7:00 AM	Shower
7:15 AM	Breakfast
7:30 AM	Drive to Work
7:45 AM	Drive to Work
8:00 AM	Check email
8:15 AM	Review News
8:30 AM	Meeting
8:45 AM	Meeting
9:00 AM	Check email
9:15 AM	Review News
9:30 AM	
9:45 AM	
10:00 AM	
10:15 AM	
10:30 AM	
10:45 AM	
11:00 AM	
11:15 AM	
11:30 AM	

Figure 1: Example of 15 min Time Tracker

Excel, but you can use any tool. Track every 15 – 30 min of your day. This may take a little effort at the beginning, but it is very helpful in seeing how much time you will have for your apartment project.

In addition to your time, think about your skill sets? Are there certain types of things that you do really well? Are you good at managing projects and managing teams? Then maybe a construction or rehab redevelopment project would be good for you. If you don't have that skill set or don't have the time to do that, maybe look at a project that needs less work. Possibly you would like something where the building does not need much rehab, and you have a property manager in place who is going to run the building for you.

Understanding what you want also includes considering your relationships. Yes – relationships. Having open, honest conversations with your loved ones before you begin investing is very important.

We have seen other investors fail half-way through a deal because their wife didn't realize how much money and/or time a deal would take. This person ended up losing a large chunk of money (that someone else benefited from) all because he didn't set the correct expectations with his wife. This is not a unique story. This happens with spouses, children, or business partners. Make sure that anyone who is going to be part of the deal (directly or indirectly) is included in the initial assessment. This will save a lot of time and heartache down the road.

Evaluate Your Finances

Once you understand what you want personally, you need to do a financial assessment. Carefully evaluate how much money you have to invest and how much you could lose. Remember no deal is certain. Understand your cut-off point. Look at how long it would take to recover if something does go wrong.

There are a few goal setting tools available, but we would recommend taking a very low-tech approach to this task. Start by pulling together a summary of all of your finances. Note which accounts you can access and how. For example, at least for now, a 401K can be self-directed by rolling it over into a corporation, and a ROTH IRA can be borrowed against for certain reasons. If you are unsure about your ability to access an account, reach out to a financial advisor for additional information. You want to know how much cash you have available and what are the costs and terms for getting it.

Write this all out, not only how much money you have available, but also how much can you afford to lose.

Set Your Goals

Next, you need to think about your intentions for the property. What do you want out of the deal? Are you looking for ongoing income, a return on your investment, something you can grow into a full-time business, or one building to supplement your income? How much time do you have before you need income or before you need to recover your money from the property, hopefully for a profit?

Use your answers to these questions, plus your understanding of yourself and your finances to put together your goals for the future. Then review them with anyone who will be part of your deal (directly or indirectly). Having your goals written down will enhance your commitment to moving forward in the exciting world of apartment investing.

You will have to be totally honest with yourself. Sometimes you need to take a step back. Don't try to make your goals fit a project. Make sure that the project fits your goals. Have clear expectations and criteria of how much money and time you are willing to invest. That will drive the types of projects and properties you should be looking for.

At this point, you may be wondering how much time you should spend on this step. After all, you haven't even looked at a building yet! It is important to take your time with this step. It is a lot of fun to jump right into looking at listings, leads, and properties. It is exciting to plug in numbers and see big returns that make the projects look appealing.

Early in our investing career, we were intrigued by projects where the numbers sounded great, but they didn't really fit our time availability. We both still had corporate jobs, so we were only able to do something that was less intensive. In addition, for our first few projects, we didn't have partners, so we could only tackle things that were within our financial reach. We got creative with some of the financing to get the maximum return, but it still had to meet our criteria.

You should take a month or so to really sit down and write out your goals. No matter what your goals are, it is very important to take this step seriously. With the proper planning, you can find a property that meets your exact needs. Without it, you may be the person who lost their shirt because they were forced to sell half-way through a project. Set yourself and your family up for success by completing the proper planning before you begin.

Understanding Your Investment Options

Types of Buildings

Now you can start to think about the building criteria that would match your goals. Some things to think about include:

- The age of a building and the amount of renovation required have a huge impact on the amount of capital required. Some buildings may be new construction with low maintenance but a higher up-front cost. Others maybe 50 or even 100 years old and need major renovations that might be done up front or possibly over time.
- The location and condition of the property will impact the amount of rent collected per apartment. This affects your income and renovation and maintenance costs.
- The size and even the location of the building determine how much time it will take to manage. For example, a building in a lower income area may take more time to manage because of increased difficulties collecting the rent in a timely manner. (To get an idea of things that go into managing an apartment building, see our book _Managing Apartments for Profit – Tips and Tricks for Taking Over and Managing Apartments_ which is available at Amazon.)

All these factors will have an effect on whether you want to manage the property yourself or have a management company do it for you.

Working with a Broker

The next step, once you decide to do apartment investing based on your goals, is to find deals! There are a variety of ways to do this.

One of the best ways is using a commercial broker. A commercial broker's business is helping property owners and banks who have apartments they need to sell. They find leads and opportunities that aren't listed with a residential agent who is buying and selling single family homes for owner/occupants.

Outside of that, there is also networking, especially if you're investing in your local area. Go to investment groups. Start letting people know that you are looking for apartments. The apartment investing world is fairly small, so once people know what you are looking for, they can help you find leads to a deal.

There are also a few websites that can be helpful during this search. One good one is Loopnet.com. It is not necessarily going to give you direct leads to the right properties for you, but there are some properties you can see for free.

You can also pay to see the full listing, but an even better use of LoopNet is to see which brokers, brokerage firms and agents are actively listing the type of properties that are of interest to you. These brokers will be directly connected to multiple owners and banks with these types of properties. If you contact them, they may give you leads that are worth more than what was listed on the site.

Selecting a good broker can take quite a while. Most commercial brokers seem to have specialties. Some will be good at smaller apartment buildings, say five to 30 units. Others may deal more with bigger buildings. Some may focus on leasing rather than sales. Just because they're a commercial agent doesn't mean that they're going to have experience and connections in the type of project you're looking for.

Cast a wide net. Ask a lot of questions about the types of properties they have, and if they have any other listing. Let them know what you're looking for, and they may say, "Yeah, this is going to be a good fit. That is the type of property that comes across my desk quite often."

Finding a broker is an easy step to get stuck on. A first-time apartment investor may find it particularly difficult to make that starting phone call. You really don't know the right questions to ask. Are you going to sound like you're not sure what you should be doing? Are they going to find out that you're a novice and take advantage of you?

You will just have to try it out. Make some phone calls. The first couple, you'll probably flub your way through. We can't keep track of how many times we have made those phone calls, unsure of exactly what to say. These guys, the good ones especially, are professionals. You are a potential catch for them, so they're going to gladly talk you through the information they have about the property plus any others that might be suitable for you. You can build a relationship with them. There's no need to be afraid of the phone call.

The best way to break free is by just getting a contact and making a call. Start practicing that introduction and let people know what you're looking for. If you are very nervous, you can write out responses to some questions that you can reference during the call. This can also help you remember all your talking points if you need the extra boost.

This way, when you're talking to brokers and when you're scouting properties, you know exactly whether the project meets your criteria and you don't end up chasing every 'shiny' deal that floats across your desk. Sometimes the most beautiful looking apartments might not be the best investment just because of the price. If you're really looking for a quick of return, you might need to tackle projects where at first sight the building isn't very pretty, but you know that there's value at the back end. By establishing your goals and sticking to them, you will be better prepared to decide if a deal is a good project for you to tackle.

Some questions to ask your broker are:

- Do they represent other buildings that meet your criteria?
- What do they see as the opportunity for new owners?

Some questions your broker may ask you are:

- How much do you have to invest?
- What other projects have you done?
- What are you looking for?

By keeping your goals in mind as you talk with a broker, you can find the project that is correct for you without overpaying and getting in over your head.

Financing

The next step is the financing piece. It is important to have contact with banks, financial institutions, and potential partners. These contacts need to be started at the same time as you begin looking for deals. That way, when you do get the property under contract, you have already started the financing process.

With financing, sometimes you just need to make a lot of phone calls. As we mentioned at the beginning of this book, on our first apartment building, Alex made 27 calls to 27 different banks before we found a bank that would finance the particular kind of project we were looking for.

The best way to get started is to find out who's financing other projects like yours. If they like that class or type of building and they are comfortable financing it for other projects, that's probably a good lead for you.

Again, this is just like the brokers. Some brokers specialize in certain types of properties. Banks are the same way. They get very comfortable with certain areas or certain types of properties or ages of properties. It's not that they won't do other deals. They just know certain types of deals better than others. Then they feel more comfortable that their numbers make sense. They have confidence in them because they see that type of deal all the time.

If it's not something they do regularly, then you may want to find a different bank. For example, We would recommend you don't go to a single-family mortgage broker to see if they will finance an apartment complex.

They're not going to be able to talk through the numbers, and they may have a hard time completing the same analysis that a commercial lender would do.

When you are talking to banks, let them know what you want when you first call. Let them know that you're looking at buying an apartment building and you were wondering what their financing terms on projects like that this would be. They may send you to their real estate or commercial lending department but let them make that decision.

We have been asked if it is better to deal with local or national banks. It depends on the scale on your project. Like almost anything, you should get multiple quotes. When you're working with a vendor or a contractor, you want to get multiple quotes. When you're working with banks, you'll want to get multiple quotes. Not every bank is going to have the same terms, although they will probably be similar. More importantly, not every bank's going to have the same comfort level with your type of project.

If you're doing a smaller project, your local banks will probably be more favorable to you. If you're doing a fairly large project, you might find some national banks that would have an interest.

We have not yet done any of our financing with a national bank. The advantage of a local bank is you can build a relationship. They will grow with you as you're going from being a first-time apartment investor to a second, third, and fourth time. They will gain a comfort level with you as well as your experience and the projects you've done. This will make future deals much easier.

Financing Watch Out

One thing to be aware of when thinking about your financing is using hard money. Hard money is generally when you're going outside of a traditional bank. It is a private lender that is giving you very hard terms in order to finance your project. It's a very high interest rate, but they may help when you have an unfinanceable project.

For traditional apartment buildings, you'll typically need to be 80% occupied with a stable rental history and good cash flow for a bank to seriously consider lending to you. Hard money lenders can fill that gap.

If there is a building that is distressed, had some damage that insurance didn't cover, or maybe was just mismanaged, a bank would say, "This is not a stabilized investment for us." The hard money lender might be willing to lend on that property until you are able to get it stable. You, however, don't want to count on a hard money lender for permanent financing.

You might use their financing for 6 to 12 months while you get the property up and stabilized. Then you can go to a bank and refinance to get a stable lower interest rate loan and pay off your hard money lender.

We have not used hard money on any of our projects because it comes at a very high cost. Although it did seem we might need hard money for a couple of projects, luckily, we had already built relationships with our local lenders. They were able to finance properties that would not have met their normal underwriting criteria. They were able to stretch their guidelines because they knew us and what we could achieve with that type of property. They could see the value at the end, and they had confidence and trust in our experience. They felt we could turn this project around and make it a good, stabilized project.

For more information on financing your buildings read **SECTION 3: FINANCING APARTMENT BUILDINGS.**

Achieving Success

So far, we've talked about defining your specific goals, talking to brokers, and financing your apartment building. These are the major steps for apartment investors and especially first-time investors to follow. In order to achieve success, review these steps regularly.

Because you took the time needed for step one, you're going to have your plans and your goals in place. You already know your time and money requirements and your style of investing. Now that you've talked to brokers, looked at deals, and spoken with banks, you should go back and review your goals again. Are still looking for the correct type of deal? It is easy to drift off track once you have seen the "shiny," fancy buildings that look so appealing. Remind yourself of your investment goals and make sure that the projects you're looking at, the type of financing you're looking for, and the deals that the brokers are bringing you are really suitable for your goals. Don't let them steer you. You need to steer them.

The Best Mindset for Success

If there is one trait that every apartment investor needs to have it is determination, especially if you don't have any prior real estate experience. Be determined that you will succeed. You are going to get that apartment building, and that will move you down your path toward your investment goals.

If you are not determined, if you are not confident in it, if you are not really sure this is going to be the right move for you, then you will not be successful. There will be times when it is frustrating. We've had many projects that have taken over a year to close, and that was after we already found the building and had it under contract. There have been times it has taken a year even to find a project that was suitable for our goals.

This leads to the second important trait, which is patience. Just remember that no matter how long it takes, as long as you're focused on your goals and determined that you're going to find something that meets those goals, you will succeed.

Time Wasters to Avoid

There are a few areas to watch out for that will waste your time without providing results. The first mistake is jumping right into looking at deals. This goes back to first clearly setting your goals.

Let's say, for example; your goal is a building that has at least a 20% upside, is going to generate at least $3,000 a month in cash flow and is going to return all of your investment in five years. Don't look at a 6-unit building that's only going to cash flow $1,000. And at the same time don't look at a 600-unit building that's going to cash flow millions of dollars, but you don't have the funds to close, you don't have the time to dedicate, and you don't have the necessary experience. Keep in mind that clear picture of what you want, and don't waste time looking at deals that are not right for you or your situation.

There will be deals that you'll look at and say, "Yeah, it doesn't meet my goals, but if it was this, this, or this, it might work." This is a big mistake.

Make sure the type of projects you look at meet all your basic criteria. Otherwise, you'll waste a lot of time looking at deals that you'll never be able to (or want to) close. Projects that are not in line with all your criteria can waste a lot of your valuable time.

Analysis Paralysis

Another time waster can be analysis paralysis.

There is a term in the investing industry that refers to people who evaluate a lot of deals but never close. It is called 'analysis paralysis.' Usually, these people have not carefully defined their criteria and therefore, are overloaded with data from all kinds of projects. This leads them to get stuck in analysis and feel they never have enough information to move on. They are "paralyzed" and can't move forward with picking out the buildings that might work for them.

If you have followed the steps listed here, this should be less of a risk because you will only be looking at properties that meet your criteria.

The Biggest Challenges

There are a lot of challenges for apartment investors. The real estate world as a whole, and definitely apartments, can change a lot from year to year. When we bought our first apartment building, it was shortly after the real estate crash of 2008 in early 2009. The advantage was prices had gone down. The disadvantage was there were a lot of banks that weren't lending. There were many banks that were getting consolidated or closing shop, and there were also a lot of banks that just flat out weren't financing apartments. They'd gotten burned on overleveraging and overfinancing buildings, so they would no longer do apartment building or commercial loans.

Several years later, the challenge can be that real estate is doing very well. There is a lot of competition. There are many people that want to invest in apartments. The price of apartments has gone up. There are not as many deals, and there are not nearly as many opportunities to buy.

In this market, many owners are getting rent increases, which is good. Occupancy is high, which is good. That also means owners are less motivated to sell. It can be especially tough to find someone who's willing to sell at a reasonable price. That is why you must analyze your deals and understand your goals, so you don't overpay on a project. Remember patience until you find what you are looking for.

As you can see both up and down, markets have advantages and challenges. The trick is managing the challenges and using the advantages. There are opportunities in every market condition.

A HUGE Overlooked Opportunity

A challenge for investors is seeing the potential of projects. Many buildings can do much better than what their current numbers indicate. Our business strategy is to find a property that can be improved, as opposed to just buying it for what it's currently doing and hoping to run it that same way.

While keeping things the same as they were is a strategy for some people, we think the biggest opportunity is looking at the potential. How much could you improve this building's performance if you change management or some of the maintenance programs or do some renovations? Is there a way that the current rent could be higher? Could the vacancy rate or expenses be lower? These are areas that some apartment investors may not think about improving. For more information on how to improve your property and increase your profits, you can read our book _Managing Apartments for Profit – Tips and Tricks for Taking Over and Managing Apartments,_ which is available at Amazon.

Apartment Investing Case Study

We have seen many examples of exactly what we have been talking about. We have known short-term investors who didn't follow the steps listed and are now back to their corporate jobs. We have known want-to-be investors who haven't even started because they have no idea what they are looking for or how much they can invest in time and money.

All our projects from our first building to our most recent purchase have followed the path that is outlined here.

One example is a property we closed on where the building met our criteria but required a lot of determination and patience. We had been looking for nine months since our prior deal before we found this one. It took us three months to get the property under contract and another six months to get it from contract to close. (Standard is about a 3-month close). The whole time, we continued to analyze how well it would meet our goals, including our financing requirements. We had to be patient but keep focused and determined to make sure the deal went through and matched our criteria.

It really does take looking at a lot of deals in order to find the 'right one.' There is a statistic that says for every 100 deals you evaluate you will generally only get 1 to close. We don't know if it's really 100 deals that you should be looking at, but you do need to review many opportunities before you find the one or two that will meet your specific investment goals.

Of course, you have already reduced that number because you were able to communicate your needs to your broker clearly. It takes time, but if you review a large number of deals, know your financing, and really understand your goals, you can find the right property and be truly successful.

Time Management Tips

When apartment investing, a great way to save your time is to use other people's time and resources. That is a big reason to use commercial brokers.

Commercial brokers are out in the real estate world every day. Their job is to help you buy a building. They talk to banks about projects that may be coming up or maybe in trouble. They talk to owners, people that may want to buy, people that may want to sell and people that have bought and sold in the past.

Apartment investing is different from single-family real estate because there is very little that ends up being held for someone's lifetime. Some people may buy a duplex or a fourplex, finance it for 30 years, and own it for 30 years. A lot of apartments, however, may have been purchased five or 10 years ago, but now the owner's goals or strategies have changed, and they are ready to sell.

Brokers are constantly out there using their time and energy networking, contacting, finding leads. Make sure that you utilize that. Use their resources, time, and skills to help you find your building, so you are not on your own trying to find that one perfect building.

Final Thoughts on Laying Your Foundation

To get motivated, remember that investing in apartments can be an amazing opportunity. Alex was able to go from a well-paid corporate job to well-paid self-employment fairly quickly. We started eight years ago, and it was only three years from our first building until Alex left the corporate world. The scale, the return on investment, and the chance to run it like a business can lead to a very successful future. You just need to get out there and be determined that you will find a great deal. The best part is once you find that first one, the second one is much easier.

Once again, you need to know what you're looking for, have a funnel for leads on deals, and get your financing in place. If you have those three pieces of the puzzle, then you're going to find the investment opportunity that's right for you.

If you have already decided that apartment investing is the thing for you, then you have made a great decision. We think it's an excellent investment vehicle, and a great way to achieve personal and financial goals.

We hope, now that you have read this section, you have a much clearer understanding of the foundations of apartment investing. You are now on the road to huge success!

SECTION 2:

BUYING YOUR BUILDING

The TRUTH About
Evaluating Apartment Deals

How We Learned the Ropes

Within the world of apartment investing, we have done many different projects. Some were very large, and some were small, some were really easy, and some were very difficult. Each one was unique and required a thorough evaluation to ensure that it was an appropriate deal for our portfolio.

To complete all these deals, we have gone through hundreds of evaluations of possible purchases. It is impossible to keep track of how many deals we have evaluated because many never even make it past the first step. The numbers and logistics can show pretty quickly if it is not the right deal, so you spend very little time on that evaluation. On the other hand, there have been quite a few; we have taken much further.

With our overall and individual property visions, we have been very successful. On our very first deal, we recovered all our cash back out of the project within about nine months. We continue to own the building, and still, get cash flow from it. We were able to recoup that initial investment and then roll it into more projects.

Other projects take much longer. A perfect example is a smaller 24-unit building. It had quite a few management problems and some outdated systems. We evaluated it, figured out what we could do to improve the property, and get new systems in place. It needed furnaces, all new windows, some of the plumbing, and updates to the kitchens and bathrooms. We did a full renovation, increased all the rents, moved in new tenants, and reoccupied the building. This greatly improves its performance.

It took about 12 months to improve and re-tenant the building. The purchasing of the building took much longer. We pursued it for 6 months and took another 6 months to close, but we wanted that building because it was directly across the street from another property we already owned, making it more convenient to manage. Overall, it was almost a two-year process from the time we first looked at the building until we finally had it done, closed, rehabbed, reoccupied, and stabilized.

Part of the challenge with apartment investing is that it can be a longer-term process. You need to know what you want out of it so, as you're evaluating each deal, you have a clear vision of where you're going.

We have been very successful, but it has taken a lot of projects over the years to get us where we are today and allow Alex to have this as his full-time occupation. He now manages this as a business with a full team including a maintenance crew, and office staff. It's been very successful, but it took time to learn the ropes and how to prevent mistakes along the way.

The information and real-life examples we share in this book should help you find success more quickly and easily and give you a head start in your apartment purchasing efforts. For more information on getting started from the ground up read the above *Section 1: Foundations for Success.*

Secret #1: Don't Trust the Pro Forma

Your first question is probably "What is pro forma?" Pro forma is the information a broker or seller will put together that will say what a building could do. They'll plug in potential rents, they'll plug in potential expenses, they'll plug in basically the best-case scenario of what this building could be. This is what could be, NOT what is.

Do not make the mistake of buying a property based the pro forma information that you get from a broker or from a seller. There's a phrase that says, "Buyers are liars, and sellers are worse." This is not what the property is actually doing today. So that is the first and biggest secret – do not put too much trust into the pro forma statement. The building may be able to perform that way, but probably not without a lot of work.

Income & Expenses • 50 Units

Pro Forma on Current Rent Roll	Keokuk / Bamberger		Income/Expenses Sep 16 - Aug 17	Total
# of Units	50		# of Units	50
Income	$367,800		Income	$310,925
8% Vacancy	-$29,424		Expenses	
Adj Gross	$338,376		Landscaping	$3,020
			Pest	$1,680
Expenses			Insurance	$13,983
Landscaping	$3,020		Management	$32,918
Pest	$1,680		Repairs	$35,284
Insurance	$13,983		Taxes	$13,067
Management	$27,070		Electric	$6,816
Repairs	$35,284		Gas	$4,448
Taxes	$13,067		Sewer	$13,244
Electric	$6,816		Water	$7,736
Gas	$4,448		Trash	$4,000
Sewer	$13,244		Professional	$700
Water	$7,736		Total Expenses	$136,896
Trash	$4,000		Net Income	$174,029
Professional	$700			
Total Expenses	$131,048			
Net Income	$207,328			

Figure 2: Pro Forma and Actuals from a Real Deal

The very first thing you've got to do is get actuals. Get actual rent collected, and actual expenses. Are they paying too much for utilities? Are they going way too high on maintenance? Is the building really dated so it has a lot of repair expense or maintenance costs? Are they having high turnover? Unless they give you actual numbers, you'll never know how the building is performing today.

The information in figure 1 is from a building that we were selling. This was the information that our broker was providing to interested investors.

Now you may be wondering how you get the actuals. When you're working with a broker do you ask them up front, or is this something you do after you've determined this is a project you wish to pursue? It depends. Some brokers will send both together right at the beginning as you can see in Figure 1.

Sometimes you must request the actual information to get the history. you're going to want to ask for the actual historical figures, and current rents.

You can say to them, "Look, I need the actual historical information for this property." As far as the rents, the term you'd ask for is "rent roll." That will give you the list of all the units and what they're currently rented for. That way someone won't say "Oh, these could be a thousand dollars a month," on the pro forma statement, but they are currently only renting for $800 because they haven't updated the kitchens and bathrooms, or other things.

Any broker who knows what they are doing should be able to get this information for you. No one should be listing or trying to sell a building without having the actual information. You may take a first pass at the pro forma just to see if it's the type of building you're looking for, but you really can't do a good evaluation until you have the historical information, and the existing rent roll.

When requesting the actual information, you will need a minimum of one year of actuals. That may be a the prior consecutive (also called trailing) 12 months, or it could be a prior calendar year, or the prior fiscal year. However, it is given, the bare minimum you should see is 12 months.

The biggest reason you want at least a year is there are certain bills like property taxes and insurance that only get paid once a year. If the period you see does not happen to include those bills you may think "Wow, this building's doing really well," but you are missing two large bills. Therefore, you've must see at least 12 months.

Ideally you would want to see longer, especially if it's a fairly stable property and you are expecting to take it over and run it as is. You want to see how long they have been able to maintain this history.

If it's a project you're expecting to do work on where you know you're going to change a lot of things, more than a year back is not as important, but you need at the minimum a full year's history.

Your bank will also want the actuals as part of their evaluation process. Both you and your bank will want to know, "Has this property consistently performed the way that it is today or, has it been inconsistent? Are there odd spikes or changes in the rent, expenses, or repairs?" Then you can ask questions about the discrepancies.

Another reason to ask for more historicals is sometimes when sellers know they're going to sell they might try to cut back on repair expenses to make their numbers look better, but the downside is that then they are deferring maintenance. You may take over a building where rather than replacing a furnace when it went bad, they put a band-aid on the problem. You want to get a longer history that would indicate "Hey, your repairs were running much higher two, three years ago. This last year looks really great, but it is a manipulated number." So, the more history you can get the better. At a bare minimum you must get 12 months.

This is so important that first-time buyers should almost never buy a building that does not have a 12-month history. When you ask for 12-month historicals, someone might say, "Oh we just fixed up this building. We're going to move everybody in and here's how it will perform." It can be easy to be misguided by someone saying "Yeah, it'll absolutely do this," but without that history everyone is just guessing at how the building will do. Especially for first-time buyers, we would steer away from anything that doesn't have the history

You may be wondering what someone should do if they've fallen into the trap of believing that the pro forma is good. How can they get out and back on the right track? Unless you have already purchased the building, you still have plenty of time. Even if you've gone so far as writing an offer and getting the building under contract, during your due diligence period you should be able to get the actual historical information. With this new information you can still go back and renegotiate saying, "Hey, this is not performing the way I was expecting."

The easiest way to keep yourself on track is to make sure to remember you're buying a business, and to make sure you know how that business is actually performing.

Don't buy or spend much time on an evaluation without having the actuals in your hand as a basis. Do not be shy about asking for the information.

By the way, almost all pro forma will be called "pro forma" but they might also be called "typical" or maybe even "expected" or "projected." They'll project forward what the building might do this current year, but you should always be able to get how did over the last 12 months.

Once you get their actuals, remember this is only the starting point. When evaluating a property deal and looking at the pro forma and the actual numbers, sometimes you can see a number where you say, "I know for this type of building this maintenance number is very low even in your actuals," and inflate your evaluation to something you see as more realistic. It might be they have been running at a lower maintenance cost because they're not doing the repairs that they should do, or you would do, as a new owner.

You want to plan ahead if you think you will have a higher or lower management fee, or if you're going to have higher maintenance and repairs, or lower maintenance and repairs. In some cases, you might actually lower your expected cost based on what you are projecting your operation can do. You are buying the building as a business. When you start plugging in your expected numbers and expenses, be sure to consider not only what they've been doing, but also what you expect to do. Be sure you plug in what your operational costs are going to be.

In some buildings you might not plan on updating the property. If this is your plan, the future projections and the history might be almost the same. In other buildings you may say, "All right, this is a property that is underperforming so we're going to fix these certain things so there'll be less maintenance cost. We are also going to give them newer kitchens and bathrooms so there will be less turnover." You plan that out. "I will be spending this much on expense up front, but then ongoing my maintenance cost will go down and my turnover will go down." This means you evaluate the history to come up with a purchase value, and then you conduct an evaluation for the future to determine if it is the right deal for you.

In summary, remember "Buyers are liars, and sellers are worse." That's not saying everyone's intentionally lying, or intentionally trying to manipulate or hide things. Just take their information with a grain of salt. Someone's trying to sell you their assets, so they're going to paint the rosiest picture they can. Therefore, make sure you get accurate and actual information.

You can also think of this as trust but verify. Make sure you are verifying that what they are giving you is accurate. If it's accurate and you do your own evaluation, then you are going to be successful because you'll know that you're not overpaying, under offering, or missing anything in the evaluation of the property.

Also keep in mind that even if the actual numbers are not great you still might make an offer based on your analysis of what you plan to do in the future. Basically, you do a dual evaluation. You evaluate the history to see what's it worth today and you evaluate your projections to see what it could do. Then make your decision based that information.

Actually, part of our strategy is to buy underperforming projects and then improve their performance for an increase in income and/or value of the asset.

Secret #2: Don't Worry About Why the Seller is Selling

The second secret is that you don't need to know why the seller is selling. That is the biggest question we hear when we talk to first-time apartment investors, or newer investors. They really want to know why the seller is selling because they feel like having that knowledge will help them understand whether the property makes any sense.

This could not be further from the truth. People will sell for a wide variety of reasons. There might be a bigger motivation depending on why they're selling, but that really shouldn't impact your actual evaluation as your looking at the building. Again, the building is a business. You should be basing your offer on the building's actual performance and its actual history. A lot of people want to know "Well, if this building is performing so well, why in the world are they selling it? There must be something wrong. There must be something they're hiding from me. There must be something else."

People go through changes in their investment goals that might drive them to sell. Maybe they're at a change in life where they want to sell. Maybe they want to invest in a different project so they're selling it off to get some cash for the new project. Their motivation should not fall on your list when you're looking at evaluating the property.

Look at the current performance. Look at the evaluation to know what it is worth to you, and what you should be paying. Their motivation will only impact you once they receive your offer and you see their reaction. Don't base your offer on their status or their situation.

We believe that people who spend too much time focusing on why the seller is selling, are being held back. It is an easy distraction from doing the work of getting the historical information, plugging it in and seeing what your expenses, cash flow and production are going to be. Rather than sending offers they say, "Well, this property or this owner really isn't that motivated," or "There's something wrong with that building," or "There's something wrong and that's why their selling."

Many people just assume "Well why in the world would you ever sell a building that makes money?" There are many reasons to sell a building that is making money. We have sold numerous buildings that were very profitable, but we were moving into a different investment, or we had completed the project. We knew our exit strategy going in and, in some cases, we intentionally planned only to keep a building for a set number of years. The intention all along was to sell it and go on to something else.

Sometimes people think that knowing why the seller is selling will help them find out if they're getting a good deal. Some people assume that apartment buildings are much like your own house or your own belongings. If you're going to sell them, it's because you are sick of them or maybe something is broken. You might sell because "I'm tired of the maintenance on this house," or "I'm tired of dealing with this," whatever it may be. They put a lot of emotion into their selling and buying decisions.

Do not base any purchase on emotions – either yours or theirs. There certainly are some homeowners that have a lot of emotion tied to their properties but for apartment buildings it should be a business investment to help you achieve your investment goals. This should not be an emotional purchase and most of the time it should not be an emotional sale.

If somebody has been tied up with asking and questioning about why someone is selling and has been derailed by this activity, there are a few ways to get back on track. The easiest way is to remind yourself that it's a business.

Think about it as if you're buying or selling a stock. It is an investment you're making. You want to buy the stock because you think it's going to appreciate in value, or be very stable, or whatever your goals are to meet your investment criteria.

When you're ready to sell it, it's probably made its investment goal for you. When you go to sell that stock, the person buying from you doesn't try to find out your ulterior motives for selling the stock. Look it from that perspective. Remove the emotion because hardly anybody has an emotional attachment to individual stock investments.

You're investing in a business so keep your brain focused on the business transaction. You need to understand the business performance. You need to understand your business plan. You need to understand your investment goals for this business and take all distractions out of the picture. People are buying and selling businesses all the time to fit their investment strategies and goals. Don't get too hung up on the idea that if someone's selling there must be something wrong. Don't spend time or worry about why the seller is selling.

Secret #3: You Can Change the Property

The third secret ties to the last two. Many people think that whatever the last owner did is all that can be done with the property. Be careful because the idea that the future performance of the property won't change, can greatly impact your investment career in both a good and bad way.

When you're evaluating the deal, you may miss an opportunity because you'll say, "Oh this building is performing terribly. There's no way I ever want to invest in a property like that because it's not performing. It can't meet my investment goals."

Well, maybe there's something you can change that would help you achieve your goals. One huge window of opportunity is appreciation in the value of the property. Another way to get a return on your investment is to take an underperforming asset and make it a better performing asset.

Conversely there's the opposite side where the building has been doing really well, and you assume "Well it will run exactly the same way once I get it." If you don't pay attention to their current management program and how they're running the building, when you get in there, if you do not run it the same way, your performance might go down. Now you have over paid for the property because you can't make it run the same way as the last owner.

Either way you can miss an opportunity. You might underestimate what it can do and miss the chance to take a poorly performing property and turn it into a money maker, or you might overpay if you cannot get the same high level of performance as the prior owner.

We have a real-life example of a first-time investor making this mistake with dire results. We sold a property that we had been able to run really well. It was in a lower income area. It was an older building. It was built in the 1920's or 1930's, so it was a 70-year-old building. It was a three-story building with no elevators, so it was a walk-up which also made renting and collecting rent more difficult.

It was a difficult property to manage. It had fairly high tenant turnover. It was all one-bedroom apartments so there were not a lot of stable renters. With one-bedroom apartments you generally have higher turnover than with two bedrooms. Also, in a lower income area you're going to have higher turnover.

We managed the building very closely and tightly, so we were on top of collections, and maintenance. We had a lot of communication with the residents to make sure we were fixing maintenance issues or fixing any problems that happened in the building. Addressing them immediately so that when someone left the apartment was ready to go, and we could get somebody moved in quickly.

The person we sold it to was not a very experienced owner and assumed they could run it the same way. We manage our own buildings, so we are closely engaged. He hired a management company to handle the property that wasn't used to working in that area, nor did they have any experience with that style of building. His management company was not as engaged, did not have clear communication with the tenants, were not good at fixing the maintenance items and were slow to release the apartments. He soon had a high vacancy rate, poor collections, and a very expensive management system.

When he purchased the building, he didn't account for his change in management style. He assumed he would get the same results we had shown. He ended up buying a property that did not meet his investment goals because he overestimated the future performance under his operating plan.

There are two main steps that we recommend to first-time apartment investors to help them to make sure they don't make the same mistake as that gentlemen did.

The first is to get the actual historicals, get the financials like we talked about before. Based on that you can see how the building is performing, and where they are spending their money. Then compare this with how you are planning to manage the building.

Then the second piece is pay attention to comparables. What makes sense? Look at a variety of buildings to see how this building compares to others. Does it match how other buildings are performing in the area? Does it match how other buildings are performing for its age, and for its type of construction, or for its unit type? If it's not in line with the others, then evaluate why it is different. There is probably some reason this building is not matching the others. Consider this discrepancy because once you take over that could either change for the better, or it could change for the worse.

If the building you are evaluating has expenses that are running much higher than the other buildings around the area, then there's probably an opportunity there to fix something or change something that could drive that down. If the expenses seem unusually low, it's the same thing. There's probably something that's being hidden or maybe some maintenance that's not being done. There is something that's artificially deflating that.

Unfortunately, the only way of knowing that is just diving in and doing a lot of evaluations comparing buildings in your area because different areas of the country have different expenses. In the North there's a lot of utility costs for heat in the winter, and salt and snow removal. But in the South, you'll have more expenses in the summer for your air conditioning and various other things. You need to make sure you're comparing similar buildings, similar construction, and similar areas so that you can accurately compare the numbers to see what makes sense and what doesn't.

Secret #4: Know Your Exit Strategy Before You Begin

It is absolutely critical to know your exit strategy from the beginning of a project so you can evaluate how the property is doing today and how it's going to do for you in the future based on your exit strategy.

From Section 1: Foundation for Success, you know the importance of goal setting to make sure that you have determined your long-term plans for the property. Are you going to sell it? Are you going to refinance it? Are you going to hold onto it for a really long time? Whatever your strategy, make sure you use that as your frame of reference as you're projecting forward. You are evaluating, "Does the property make sense if I keep it for X number of years and then sell or refinance it to get my cash back."

Everybody needs to have their own exit strategy that meets their individual needs and situation. We have used the exit strategy of buying something, fixing it up, selling or refinancing it three to five years later and then doing that again. With our strategy of holding it for five years, we only plan for the short-term needs which has really allowed us to grow

On the other hand, a friend of ours deals with smaller buildings and his game plan is to buy a building, fix it up and hold it for 20 or 30 years. In his projections, he understands that during those 20 to 30 years he will need to start replacing roofs, updating kitchens and upgrading the units. So, he has factored all of that in when he does his initial planning. Because he knows that is his exit strategy, he is better able and more prepared to deal with those expenses as they come up.

Your goals need to tie to your exit strategy, and your goals and your exit strategy need to match the building. We have purchased some buildings knowing what we can do with them to turn them around, increase their value and sell them. If our intention was to do what our friend has done and hold a building for 30 years, some of the buildings we have purchased would not have been appropriate because they were not good buildings to hold on to for 30 years. There could have been numerous long-term repair and maintenance costs. It would not have made sense for our rapid growth strategy.

However, the same buildings we passed on might have made sense for a different investor who was looking for stable cash flow once they were fixed up. So, everyone has different goals. This goes back to understand why someone is selling and if a property doesn't make sense for one person why it would make sense for somebody else. It is all about different goals and different exit strategies.

In summary, you might want a property you can keep for 20 years for the monthly cash flow. You know it's not a huge check, but it's stable and consistent. Others of you may want to be more aggressive pursuing projects with a high return rate so you can get cash back within a couple years to do another project.

These two types of investors will look at the same project in very different ways. It might be perfect for one person and not suitable for another. Just make sure you understand your investment goals and your exit strategy as you evaluate each deal.

An Actual Apartment Evaluation Story

We have a perfect example that sums up what we've been talking about. It is one of our favorite properties, but it was a lengthy process to purchase.

It is a 40-unit apartment complex and our original information included the pro forma information. The pro forma projected every 2-bedroom unit renting for $800, and $600 rent for one-bedroom units. The pro forma made this building look like it was performing great and would be a fantastic deal. We liked the location and thought the building sounded good, so we decided, "It's worth looking at. Let's get the actuals from the seller."

Then they sent over an actual of their trailing 12-month performance. Their actual rents were about $200 less per unit than what the pro forma showed.

So, based on that we knew a few things. First, it wasn't worth what they were asking because it wasn't performing the way they were implying that it was. In addition, we realized that in our future performance projections there was probably room for growth if we could bring it up to their pro forma level.

Based on this information, we were able to make a lower offer more in line with the existing performance. We knew we could improve this building's performance and we didn't really care why they were selling.

It was a clean building and was fairly well maintained. They were clearly not getting the maximum possible rents. We did not allow ourselves to get distracted by why they were selling. We made a fair offer based on the existing performance and were able to close on the purchase.

Once we owned the building, we updated some kitchens and bathrooms and did some minor cosmetic repairs. We set up a much more involved management team that made sure rents were collected on time, vacant units were re-rented quickly, troublesome tenants were removed in a timely manner and followed other good management practices. For more information on management see our book ***Managing Apartments for Profit,*** now available at Amazon.

With these changes we were able to increase rents on average $200 a unit, to almost exactly what they showed in their pro forma. We were able to get an asset that was underperforming, buy it based on its actual performance, improve that performance and then benefit from that higher return. We increased the cash flow and increased the value of the project which can be used to either refinance, taking out cash, or selling for a profit.

It was a fantastic deal and has been one of our favorite projects.

Secret #5: Different Methods for Changing Times

In a Hot Market Deals Happen Much Faster

One of the many things that can change in the apartment market is timing. There are times when there is no rush to make a deal. Multiple properties in almost the same area and condition might be listed for six months before getting an offer. When transactions are not happening that quickly, you can think about it for a few days and really dive into the evaluation.

Then there are times when apartment investing heats up. There are a lot more investors getting into the market, but the good news is there are also more banks willing to lend on apartments.

If the project makes sense, people will make an offer and aggressively pursue it. In this competitive market you can't take too long. We have seen a couple deals that were on the market for only a week before they were under contract. Therefore, when you're doing your evaluation you don't have to rush, but you "don't have all day."

To speed up your analysis it helps to be aware of a couple of traps that can slow you down. One common trap is "analysis paralysis" which we discussed in Section 1. Don't get distracted by doing too much analysis or playing with the numbers. Know your goals and how to get the correct information so you can quickly complete your evaluation. If, based on your evaluation, it seems appropriate, you can say, "Yes, this is a property that interests me," and keep moving forward. That way you don't miss out on the opportunity.

In this book we have shown you some specific tips to help you evaluate deals thoroughly, quickly and with a clear head. Analysis paralysis is really a state of mind. You may be so focused on the analysis you cannot proceed forward with any deal, and therefore lose out on all of them. You can't make a decision because you want to be sure you know all the numbers and have them exactly right. In addition, your contract should include due diligence time so you will have an opportunity for further evaluation after the building is under contract and before closing. (See below for more on this.)

Analysis paralysis is also a convenient distraction for people who aren't ready to commit. If they stay focused on analysis and the evaluation phase, then they never have to actually purchase a project.

At some point you need to decide if you're investing and move forward. Assuming you have already decided that you want to be an apartment investor, then consider, "does this project make sense?" It is important to do a thorough evaluation, but you need to put in an offer in order to become an investor.

If you find yourself stuck in analysis paralysis, there a few steps you can take to help get out of that cycle.

The biggest thing is to stay focused on your goal. Your goal is not to evaluate buildings. Your goal is to invest in buildings. Keep in mind that you're never going to get any sort of return if you are not actually investing. It may be a fun project to evaluate apartments, but if your goal is to invest in apartments and get a return on that investment, you will never get there until you actually buy a property.

Always keep your eye on the final goal. Make sure you're very clear that you are going to invest in apartments. Don't let yourself get distracted. If a deal doesn't make sense, then move on. If there's something not right about it, kick it to the side and move on to the next one. There are plenty of opportunities out there for investments. Don't get too bogged with the evaluation, and don't get stuck trying to make a particular deal work.

Another problem is wasting a lot of time by getting too detailed. Even though we are telling you to get the accurate and actual information, some people try to go too far in the initial evaluation. As you write your offer, you need to include time in your contract to do due diligence.

Once someone accepts your offer and you have it under contract, then, with your due diligence clause, you will have a chance to gather more information like copies of the leases and actual maintenance contracts. If you find anything that mismatches, you can go back to the seller and say "Hey this didn't match what you told me before. This would have changed my offer price," and you can renegotiate, or ask for a concession or change. That's what that due diligence window is for. You don't need to answer 100% of the questions in the initial evaluation step because you are going to have some additional time after you have it under contract.

When you're doing the initial evaluation, you only need enough information to know if the property is a good fit for you and meets your investment goals. If the answer is yes, then you pursue it and put in an offer. Don't get distracted by trying to get too much detail at the very front end.

Time management and persistence will also help. The best tip for managing your time during the evaluation process is to be consistent. Gather the information including the actuals, and consistently, for every project you are considering, plug the numbers into your spreadsheet. It may take several potential projects to get comfortable knowing if a deal meets your goals but eventually you will get better at making that determination.

It is easy to get distracted trying to make one particular deal make sense. A lot of investors, particularly first-time apartment investors, really want a deal. If they are having a tough time finding the deal, they start trying to force deals to match their goals. This is a very bad way to approach a project and will lead to making poor decisions. Forcing a bad deal to work just to have something in your portfolio could lead to disastrous consequences.

Just consistently evaluate and gather the information on various properties to see if they will meet your goals. If you keep plugging away eventually you will find the project that does meet your goals and investment strategies. Then you can move on that deal.

Once you find one that works, you can use that as your template. Don't waste your time looking at large variety of deals once you have an idea of what matches your needs. Knowing your goals and evaluating deals consistently, will give you the biggest reward for the least work.

When Prices are Going Up

One challenge for investors is when prices are increasing and there is more competition. That doesn't mean there aren't any deals out there, they're just a little harder to find.

First this means that you need to understand your goals and criteria so you can do a quick evaluation and not miss out on good deals.

This also means that as more people are investing and prices are going up, you must pay very close attention to whether a deal still makes sense for you.

Some return rates may be smaller than they had been in the past but there are positive returns and value out there. There are still good investment deals. In some cases, you might have to pay a bit more than you would have liked but if you are still getting a return that makes sense, you might make the offer.

It is important to remember that the market is cyclical. There are very clear market cycles that occur. Eventually this higher priced cycle will begin to turn down. There are a lot of factors that can influence this change, and it also could be very regional. Some parts of the country may hit the top first and begin a decent while other areas are still going up. This is hard to tell and very hard to predict.

This shouldn't dissuade you from investing in real estate because the market will always be going up and down. For buyers it is ideal to buy when the market is down. However, since you are buying a business when you buy an apartment building, you are able to invest any time. We continue to invest in both high- and low-priced markets.

As long as you are buying something that will be profitable for you, then, even if the market takes a dip, you are still able to pay your bills and have some cash flow. That is why it is so important to conduct a thorough analysis and understand what you are buying on the front end. Then you know, if the market does dip, you are more protected than someone who bought a building without understanding how it will perform for them. You will be in a much better position, and perhaps even able to buy something else before the prices go back up.

Secret #6: Tools and Resources to Be Careful With

Beware of Online Tools

There are some online tools that are giving misleading information. Zillow, and other web resources give evaluations of properties or estimated values that may not be not keeping up with the times.

Especially with apartments, a lot of transactions aren't on the Multiple Listing Service (MLS) the way a house would be. Most properties are listed through individual brokers. Some tools that gather information online from public records, and from offerings at various websites don't see all these properties. Also, there are often not enough comparable apartment buildings to accurately determine a price.

These online sites have their analytics tool that says, "Oh I've seen six houses sell in this neighborhood for $300,000 a piece so this house is going to be worth $300,000 too." When these tools try to do that same thing with apartments, there aren't six apartment buildings all within one neighborhood that are selling for a certain price.

You cannot evaluate apartments buildings the same way you would evaluate your house. The tools are not the same, and the analysis is not the same. So, stay away from those tools unless your goal is to focus on single-family home or smaller unit buildings, like 5-units or less. With apartments we have found online tools can be incredibly inaccurate and inconsistent in their evaluations.

For those of you who are focusing on apartment buildings, you will need to use your own analysis to determine the value of the property. This analysis is based on the historical information, and the performance of the property. That is what really drives the value, not so much a sales comparison.

With apartment buildings value is highly dependent the cash flow, expenses and rent roll. You might have two buildings that are directly across the street from each other with vastly different values because of how they are performing. Therefore, you've must make sure you use their actual performance for your evaluation and don't just guess based on what other things around it are worth or have sold for.

Be careful if the Management Company Is Also Involved in Selling the Property

We have heard about some people who buy buildings from a management company and then turn around and hire that management company to manage the buildings. Earlier we mentioned the importance of knowing how the building has performed and how it could perform. In this case you don't have an independent perspective like you would if you had your own management company. When they're telling you how the building could do, or how the building has done, it might be slightly misleading information because they are motivated to sell the property.

Buying from a management company and then keeping that management company for the property seems to happen more often with people that are out of state and don't know the area. It also often happens with smaller properties like single families, duplexes, and four families. Unfortunately, all the times we have seen this happen, the buyers significantly overpaid. The property did not perform the way the buyer thought it would. Even if the management company says "If you buy it, we'll manage it for the first year for free" if the management performance isn't there, the buyer did not get a good deal.

We are not trying to say that all management companies will do this, or that this arrangement is necessarily a bad thing. Just be extra cautious during the analysis if this is something you are considering. If the person that's selling the building is also going to manage it, there could be a conflict of interest. They are biased in their opinion as they're giving you information.

Be Careful of a Commercial Broker That Represents Both Buyer and Seller

A lot of people ask about having a broker who is on both sides of the deal. When we refer to someone being on both sides of the deal, we mean the broker represents both the seller and buyer in the same deal.

For a first-time investor especially, it is important to have your own broker to help you find deals for you to evaluate. This broker is focused on helping you get what you want.

It might be that your broker who is representing you as the buyer also happens to have a listing to sell that matches your criteria. In that case they would be on both sides and with ethical brokers that is probably not a problem. It can be an issue if they are an unethical broker. and that is why it's important to have, as a buyer, your own broker.

If your broker brings you at least some leads that they don't represent as the selling agent, you can feel fairly confident that they're ethical. They're not trying to steer you towards something just because they would get a higher commission. If they are only giving you leads where they are the listing agent or broker, we would be pretty cautious. It sounds like they are only going for the highest commission and not focused on meeting your needs.

When you have a broker that's representing you and helping you find properties, if they're showing you properties from multiple resources and you happen to buy something where they also represent the seller, that can be fine. Just be aware and be cautious.

Secret #7: Resources and Tools to Use

The Best Resources Any Apartment Investor Should Use

Having the right team of resources is very important for real estate investors. As you are doing your evaluations, there are three resources that are particularly important. These are management companies, banks and commercial brokers because these are the most helpful in understand how a building can run.

A lot of first-time investors decide to use management companies, and this is not a bad idea. If you have a day job or other things that are going to take your time, hiring a management company can help you to be successful.

If your goal is to be a hands-off investor and have a management company manage your building, knowing what a management company costs, what type of buildings and in which locations it has experience managing, will be critical to your evaluation.

If you plan to hire a company, make sure you have them look at the buildings with you. They should be able to tell you based on their experience if the numbers that the seller is providing make sense. How would they operate the building once they take it over? What would they project the occupancy rate, collection rate, turnover and maintenance expenses to be?

They can answer those questions for you. They have a breadth of experience that you may not have. If they're managing apartment buildings in your area, they should know how those buildings perform. They can help you gauge whether it's a good or bad building and if the numbers make sense.

If you are planning to have a management company manage your building it is critical to start talking to them before you buy the property. If you wait until you have closed on the deal, it's too late. You need to talk to them before, so they are engaged, and you know that it's the type of building they are going to be successful managing. For more information on what to do once you buy the building you can read our book ***Managing Apartments for Profit***, available at Amazon.

During your evaluation you either want to choose a management company to match the properties you are considering or choose properties to consider that match you manager.

If your management company is only used to working on properties in a certain part or area of town and you're getting something in a different area, you might need to consider using a different management company. A company that does not work much in a certain area will not be on site as often. They might not know the demographics. They might not be as familiar with, "Hey this is what the market rent would be for this building," if they don't know that market. They can't guide you as well into saying, "Wow, they're already getting the top rent for the area," or, "Well they're really under what the area rent is."
They also might not understand the clients in a new area. They might not be as good at marketing to them or understanding the management styles that will work best with them. For more information on managing

styles see our book _**Managing Apartments for Profit**_, available at Amazon

 So, it is absolutely critical to have a management company as a part of your team of resources, but it needs to be a company that matches the type of building and location you are considering.

The other resources you should be talking to are the banks because 1) they know what type of properties they're going to finance for you and 2) they can tell you how they're going to evaluate the building. If you run a building past them and say, "Hey I'm looking at this particular property, here's how I'm projecting it," you can see if that matches the way they would evaluate it.

Commercial lending departments lend on apartments all the time, so they see the history and actual performance of other buildings similar to the one that you're evaluating. They can guide you and say, "Wow that building makes sense," or "No, that really doesn't match the way we would plug in the expenses," or "We would plug in the occupancy at this rate." This gives you a guide as to whether or not you are on track.

The third resource is a commercial broker which we already talked about. If you have your own commercial broker, they are out in the market seeing the buildings, the transactions and performance. They can help you gauge if what you're projecting and seeing as expenses and collections make sense and match with the market. Those are three very good resources.

The Best Tools Any Apartment Investor Should Use

There are many tools that all real estate investors should have in their back pocket. Earlier we mentioned that Zillow is not a great tool for estimating the value of apartment buildings. Zillow, however, can be a good tool for determining rents. When you're trying to figure out what rents can be in an area, Zillow has a lot of rental listings. This information can also be gathered from websites like apartments.com or other online rental listings. These tools can be a great resource to evaluate potential rents.

When we're investing in areas that we don't know much about, or in an unfamiliar market, these tools provide a quick gauge to say "Is this property getting the rent that it should be getting? Is it high? Is it low?" A quick search for similar buildings or apartments on something like apartments.com or Zillow will show what others are asking for rent.

You can also see if they are giving a lot of concessions. If the first month or two months are free, then maybe there are some problems in that market. It might be tough for people to rent their units. If there are no concessions or marketing ploys, then that market is probably fairly stable.

Using these online tools is a great way to evaluate current rents and understand what the market is supporting. You can use this to gauge your potential rent and determine if there's an opportunity to change from the past rents. These are great tools to do a gut check when you are starting to invest or are entering a new market.

Another tool that is very useful is spreadsheet software, like Microsoft Excel. Throughout this book we have talked about "plugging in the numbers." This means putting the numbers into our spreadsheet software to help evaluate the deals. This is a great tool!

Our spreadsheet is a very basic income and expense sheet.

You want to start with your gross potential rent. This is the total you would make if all your units were at full market rents for the full 12 months. This is the would be the total potential you could collect over the year.

Then you will lose some money because there will be vacancies and turnover. Every apartment will not be rented all 365 days of the year, so you factor in a vacancy rate. The standard is 5%.

Although 5% is the standard vacancy rate, your specific rate will depend on your area. If you're in an area that has a higher turnover, lower income or where it is tougher to collect rents, you might be closer to a 7% or maybe even 10% vacancy.

Most banks will automatically factor in a 5% vacancy and you will want to include whatever rate you feel would be appropriate for the building you are evaluating. If someone is selling you a building that just happened to have had a 100% collection last year, you still need to factor in at least a 5% vacancy because you know eventually there will be a turnover. At some point somebody's going to move. So at least a 5% vacancy is what you should always be plugging in.

Your gross operating income is what you have after you back out your vacancy factor. To get this number you take your gross potential rent and multiply by your vacancy rate. (For 5% multiply by .05, for 7% multiply by .07, for 10% multiply by .10, etc.) Then subtract that number from the gross potential rent. This gives you your gross operating income which is what you actually collected (or will collect if you are still in the evaluation phase).

Then you plug in all your expenses. You will have taxes, insurance, sewer, water, trash, gas, electric and possibly other utilities, landscaping and lawn care, snow removal, and other things like management fees depending on the property. These all go into your expenses.
Your gross operating income, minus your expenses is your net operating income (NOI). That is your bottom line. That is what the building makes (or will make) that is profit. That is what you use to judge and put a value on the property.

You may have noticed that we didn't include the bank loan or interest rate. That is because not everyone will use a bank or have a loan, and the terms can be very different. When evaluating the building and determining the potential value you don't include loan information.

Using the real-life example:

Gross Potential Rent	$367,800
Vacancy Factor (8%)	− $ 29,427
Gross Operating Income	$338,376
Expenses	− $131,048
Net Operating Income (NOI)	$207,328

The next important number to understand as an investor is the capitalization rate, also known as the cap rate. The cap rate is a way to determine the value of a building and compare it to other real estate investments. It is the ratio between the cost of the building and the income generated by the building.

So, if you are looking at a building that costs one million dollars and it has a net operating income of $100,000 then that building at that time would have a cap rate of 10%. Meaning, before figuring in any loan costs, the building with that net income would be giving you a 10% return.

The cap rate can also help you determine the value of a building if you are unsure of what to pay. Every geographic area usually has a general cap rate. If you are unsure of the value of the building, you can use that area's general cap rate to determine the property value. If you are unsure what the general cap rate is in that area, real estate agents, brokers, or bankers should be able to help you figure out that number.

There are numerous ways a cap rate can change on a particular building. The value of the building could go up for numerous reasons such as general growth in the market, improvements made to the building, or neighborhood changes that make the property more valuable. If the value of the property goes up but the net income stays the same, then the cap rate will go down because the ratio of a more expensive property to the same net income will be less.

It is also possible for the cap rate to go up if the value of the property stays the same, but something happens to increase the net income. For example, maybe you do a better job of maintenance, thus making your apartments more desirable, decreasing the vacancy rate and increasing the net income.
Let's do a little math here. Let's assume you are evaluating a building that is making a net operating income of $100,000, and your area has a general cap rate of 10%. This means if the general cap rate of 10% is accurate you would expect to get a 10% rate of return. That would make the building worth one million dollars to you.

Mathematically to find this number take the $100,000 and divide by 10% (0.10), and you will get one million dollars as the value of the property. This means that if you paid one million dollars to purchase this property you should make around $100,000 a year, which is a 10% return.

If it's a more competitive market, or a very high-end property, it might be a five cap where you would expect to make 5% return. So that same $100,000 net income building would be worth two million dollars because if you pay two million dollars for it and you got a 5% return, you'd still make that $100,000. The $100,000 didn't change. The property still performed the way it performed, the difference is the return rate that investor's willing to get for that building and for that area.

Continuing the real-life example:

NOI / CAP = VALUE (OFFER)

NOI	CAP	VALUE
$207,328	5%	$4,146,560
$207,328	8%	$2,591,600
$207,328	10%	$2,073,280
$207,328	12%	$1,727,733

Microsoft Excel is the biggest tool we use. We put in the gross potential income, factor in the vacancy rate to get the gross operating income, then subtract the expenses to get the net operating income. Then we use the cap rates in the area to determine the value of the building. Your broker and bankers will be able to help you with understanding what cap rates (or expected rates of return) are for a particular area, and for a particular type of building.

For some of our buildings, we bought them at one cap rate, and because of the improvements, repairs, and work we did on the property, we actually moved the cap rate.

Someone was willing to pay a higher price for the same amount of cash flow because it was going to be lower maintenance due to how we repaired things. We fixed things and made the building perform better than before when it didn't have that same level of operation.

So that's really where we talk about big opportunities. You can change the performance of a property and therefore increase both the cash flow to get a net income increase, and also make the building more appealing, so it sells for more. The buyer is willing to pay more for the property and take a smaller cap rate because it's a more stable investment.

When we look at the cap rates it's very much like CDs from your bank. You know CDs are very secure investments, but you only get less than 1% return on them at most institutions. On the flip side, a very high-risk investment might get you 10% or 15% returns.

The cap rate is based on the risk factor and the competition in the market so that a brand-new building in a very popular area that is fully occupied might be a five cap or even a four cap. It might be a low return rate because someone says, "Boy, that's a really safe, stable investment."

In an area where the building or the area is a little older or maybe there's higher turnover or more maintenance issues with the property it might require a larger cap rate. This less desirable property would probably require more at the 8%, 9%, maybe up to a 10% return, or a ten cap.

So, you might be wondering, "Where does the loan come into play? I didn't hear you mention it during your evaluation." Apartment investing is a business. The business value is independent of how much you borrow to get the deal.

As you conduct your evaluation, if you are borrowing to purchase the property, you do need to factor in your loan and how much debt you plan to pay every month so you can see how much cash you have left to actually put in your pocket.

The value of the building, however, is based on the net operating income you determined with your calculations. Leaving out the loan equalizes the evaluation between different purchasers, so the value of the building is based on how the building is performing, not how much cash the buyer has.

But for your own investment goals, after the net operating income, you would plug in your debt service. By subtracting the amount you are paying your bank on the loan, you are getting to see what your actual cash flow may be.

On that same building we were just talking about, the magic building that makes $100,000 in net operating income, you would say "Okay, how much am I paying to my bank?" Well, if you are paying $80,000 a year to your bank. then your cash flow is only $20,000. If you're paying $70,000, then your cash flow would be $30,000. What you are paying in principle and interest to your bank is your debt service. After you pay that, the rest is the actual cash that goes back in your pocket.

So, our major tools are online sites to help estimate rents, especially if we are not familiar with an area and spreadsheets to help analyze each deal we are reviewing.

Secret #8: There Is Always Opportunity

Hot Market Opportunities and Challenges

There are some factors that make a hot market good for investors. Brokers are shopping deals and aggressively trying to get offers on properties. There are online sites like Loopnet which list commercial properties and because of the increased interest and the internet, it is a more open marketplace and easier to find apartments for sale.

There are, however, some challenges. The market is competitive, and prices are high and often going higher, which means cap rates are getting smaller. People are paying more for the same net income.

Good deals are moving quickly so you don't have a lot of time to evaluate. You have to do the analysis quickly so you do not miss out on the deal. This could lead to some people to get stuck in the analysis phase because deals are going so fast.

To deal with this you need to have a set process for recording and evaluating your numbers and make sure you are consistently looking at a variety of properties.

Slow Market Opportunities and Challenges

Slower markets give you more time for evaluation and it may be easier to get a good price. However, rents may be lower and as with all times, you need to be sure your numbers add up for making a profit.

The Biggest Opportunity is in Turn Around Projects

There are big opportunities all markets in turnaround projects with properties that are underperforming. It is hard to find a good return by buying an existing building that's already doing everything it can. There are much bigger opportunities if you're willing to go after projects where the buildings are not performing to the best of their abilities. These are not vacant buildings or new construction but buildings where a change in management practices can make a big difference.

These building usually have problems like low rents, and/or high maintenance costs and turnover rates All of these are opportunities for improvement.

Many people don't think they can change the performance of a building. Yes, you can. If you have a good management company or if you're able to manage it well yourself, you can totally change the performance of these properties to increase cash flow and get a better return.

If you change the performance of the property, and you've paid for it based on how it's currently performing, you get the benefit of more cash flow and higher value.

You get this just through better management of operations and performance. It is a huge opportunity.

Apartments are a business so you must run them like a business and run them well. If you do this, there are definitely opportunities out there and any time is a great time to be an apartment investor.

To Remember

It is critical to know and remember your goals and investment strategy plus your exit strategy as you are doing your evaluations.

Know the rate of return you need on your cash. This will help you determine how much cash you should put in and how you will get that cash back out if needed. Then you can say "All right, this is the way to get that cash back purely through cash flow, so I'm going to sit and hold the property for 30 years." Or you can ask yourself, "Do I need my money back faster? If so, I'm going to have it sell it in a certain number of years. Is there a large upside potential with this project so I could refinance and get my cash out through a refinance?"

If you keep in mind your investment strategy and your exit strategy as you're doing your evaluations, you are much more likely to meet your goals and be successful.

Stephen Covey's book called _The 7 Habits of Highly Effective People_ says that you should always 'begin with the end in mind'. That is absolutely critical. If you don't know what you are going to do with the building after you have it, you are going to make a lot of missteps and miss-guesses. The property might not match your actual goals. Even if the property makes some money, if your goal was to get all of your cash back in 2 years then a 30-year hold plan will not make sense. Understand that going into a deal, and your life will be so much easier.

Final Thoughts on Buying Your Building

You make your money when you buy. If you don't buy well, if you don't have a good strategy, if you don't know what you're doing with the building, you are much less likely to achieve your goals. You might overpay or miss opportunities. The most exciting thing about the evaluation is - **this is where you make your money**.

The other thing is, you just need to start. You may find that you will need to look at 100 deals, or 100 opportunities before you find ten that meet your goals. Then you may only get one of those closed and under contract.

You just need to be persistent and consistently be looking because there will be many projects that are not right for you. You need to weed out those that don't make any sense, focus on the ones that do make sense, and pursue them to get your investment started.

The most exciting part of the evaluation is knowing that you make all your money at this stage of the process. Once you own it, it's too late. You have already paid a price and made a purchase that may or may not meet your goals.

So, the evaluation is the fun part. You get to evaluate a property, figure out what it's worth, figure out what you can do with it, how you can make it worth more, how you will get your money back, and determine your exit strategy.

We hope that you now understand how to evaluate apartment deals so that you can achieve your goals and get better results with your apartment building purchases.

SECTION 3:

FINANCING APARTMENT BUILDINGS

How to Use Financing to Your Advantage

Our Experience in Financing Apartment Buildings

We have completed many different types of deals. Our very first multi-unit apartment project was just after the market crashed in 2009. This was the first large deal we did, and Alex had to call 27 banks before we found a bank that would finance the property.

It can take lot of determination to find a bank that will like your deal enough to support your dream especially when you are first starting and do not have a track record. In our case, add on that this was one of the most down markets in decades.

We were determined. We finally found someone that believed in us and our project, and it turned out to be a great deal. About nine months after we purchased the property, we got all our initial money back through a refinance.

We still own the property today and it continues to provide cash flow. This deal was a fantastic jump start to our career. This is an example of how important determination and creativity are when you are first starting in real estate investing.

Some people ask me if we could consider ourselves an overnight success with real estate. We don't like to say we are an overnight success, but we've certainly been very successful.

That story we just told about our first project has a very happy ending. We got all of our money back out of the deal, so we were able to reinvest into a second project. The second project we scaled up even larger. We went from a small apartment building to a mid-sized apartment building. With that deal we did some creative financing as well, so we were able to get the bank to finance the purchase of the building and 100% of the construction costs.

For us it has been a consistent, steady growth rate. This has a lot to do with how we finance each deal initially and after we own it. Every project we do, we build on the last one to get to the next one financed and going.

That being said, investing in large-scale real estate is definitely not without challenges and involves a lot of work. It, however, has been a wonderful ride and with the tips, tricks, and secrets we are about to share, hopefully you can enjoy investing in real estate and much as we do.

Secrets Every Investor Needs to Know to Get Financing

Know the Numbers

The first step is to make sure you accurately evaluate the deal and understand the numbers. When you start talking to a bank or any lender, they are numbers guys. They are going to understand

- your gross operating income,
- your expense percent and your net operating income, and
- your debt service coverage ratios or debt to income ratios.

So, make sure you understand these things and have them ready to present to your potential lenders.

If you are unsure what these are or how to determine them, we would recommend review the above **Section 2: Buying Your Building**. In that section we cover in great detail how to properly evaluate real estate deals.

Briefly, however, your project is going to have a gross potential rent, which is the total amount of rent you could collect if all units were 100% occupied and everybody paid on time and no one ever moved out. Then you're going to lose about 5% to vacancy. That will give you your gross operating income.

Next, you account for all your expenses (not counting financing). Your gross operating income minus your expenses is going to be your net operating income. The net operating income is your income before you pay for your loan.

The bank is then going to say, "All right. How much are you earning (your net income) and how much are you going to be paying us?" They will want to see that your net income is about 1.20 or 1.25 times the amount that you're paying the bank.

This is called the debt to income ratio. This means that every time you get $1.25 from the property, the bank will take $1.00, leaving you with $0.25. This ratio shows that you will make money and the bank is covered in case you overestimated your gross potential rent.

When talking to the bank you will need to make sure you understand all your numbers and where they came from. This will help ensure that you know how much funding you will need and your return rates so that both you and the bank are covered.

When talking to the bank you will say, "Here's what our net income would be. Here's the debt service I'm projecting on this project." The bank (or whatever lender you are using) will be more likely to lend if they see that there is plenty of cash flow to support the debt payments you are going to make when you're financing the property. From the bank's perspective if you can make money after debt service, that is good for you and the bank.

In retrospect, our lack of comprehension around the numbers was part of the challenge on that very first project that required 27 calls before we could get funding. We didn't understand the numbers as well as we do now. With the numbers we were sending the banks, the project income did not actually cover the debt.

We knew we were going to do things to change the building to make it run better, but what we sent the bank only showed what the building was doing at the present time. When you're doing your evaluation sometimes you know you're going to change something about the operation. You need to have your historic information as far as the current income and expense, but then, also, your projected income and expenses. You need to explain what you're going to change to make those numbers better. We just sent it to them as it was and thought that would be fine.

The bank wanted to see that there was some reason they should feel comfortable lending the required money. It is critical to show them that you will have the cash flow to pay that debt service. If you're not showing positive debt coverage of about 1.20/1.25 as explained above, you're really going to have a tough time getting financing.

This is the language banks and lenders speak so you need to make sure you understand all your numbers and know what your debt coverage ratios are. This is absolutely critical to getting financing.

Know What You Need - Will This Project Work for Me?

Before you jump into a deal, be sure the project will work for you. The best way for you to determine this is to practice your evaluations.

Every time you're evaluating a deal, plug in not just the income and expense, but plug in different financing options on the property. Play around with different scenarios. What would this project look like if you were going to finance 80% of it, 70% of it, 50% of it, whatever that may be? Then actually calculate what your debt payments would be and see where it lands you on a debt coverage amount.

That way you not only know the building is worth $X amount based on its net income but, also, you can know what your debt service coverage is and exactly how much cash is going in your pocket. You see your net income and then you pay the bank. After that, you will know what is actually left over for you out of the project.

It is important to incorporate the amount of cash you will be putting in and the financing terms with every evaluation. You start getting used to the numbers, and you can see the impact of either financing more or financing less on both your return rate and your bottom line.

The Best Tool to Use

The best tool to understand the cost of a project and your financing options is a spreadsheet software package (like Excel). Make sure to include your financing so that you can be sure you are not getting too much debt on a building, also called overleveraging. This will also help you when determining if you should pull in partners, and evaluating how much of the deal you can give away. Using this tool, you can see everyone's chunk and see how the financing stacks up.

For example, if you have a deal that will require one million dollars you will need to know where that money will come from. Will you get the traditional 80% from a bank? Will you need another 10% from a partner with the last 10% from you? If you set-up your deal in this way will you still get money in your pocket?

Do you need cash flow each month or are you ok with larger chunks of money during a refinance or sale of the building? Having a spreadsheet that outlines all your numbers and possible scenarios will help make sure that you are making the right choices for the project.

In addition, you will need to know your goals. We cover the first step of buying a property in ***Section 1: Foundations for Success***, at the beginning of this book.

Also, it is interesting to note (see the most unlikely secret below) that bigger projects may be easier to finance. If you get stuck worrying about the size of your project and the financing options, the best way to get unstuck is to talk to banks. When you are uncertain or nervous about looking at bigger projects, talk to lenders. Talk to financiers. Let them know what you're looking at. Let them know what you're thinking about getting into and see what their appetite is based on your project. You might be surprised that if you present them with a bit bigger building, they might find it more appealing.

In addition, partners may be easier to attract if you're looking at some larger deals. It is kind of exciting and it's a way to really capture people's interest.

Be Creative

The best secret with real estate investing is that it has a great ability to be creatively financed. Many investors are only used to the things they've financed before which were probably cars and houses. These generally just have a regular bank loan. There's really not much else you can do when you're buying your first house or second house or a third house or when you're buying your car. There are really no options to do anything else other than just go to the bank, put your 20% down, and now you own a house. People aren't used to thinking that there are different ways you can get financing.

With apartments, you can get very creative because it is a business. There are different ways you can bring people onboard. You can also get very aggressive with bank financing itself. This is the part in the process where creativity is very important and can be used to your advantage.

We've done deals with partners where we put down none of the cash. They put down all of the cash and we still split the deal because we were putting the project together. We were going to manage the project, so we still had an ownership stake without having any cash in it.

We have done other deals where we have two partners that are separate owners on the property. They don't own it as a single entity. You have two different entities that are co-owners on the same property with a different percentage split.

There is a wide variety of ways you can finance projects. There are construction loans plus a lot of other financing options. You can get more creative with apartments than you can with other investments because they are bigger, and they are a business.

Apartment buildings do not have the same regulations ss single family and residential financing. That lets you get more creative in finding ways to bring in partners and other people, so the deals make sense and provide a good return for everyone involved.
We had a project that we financed from a bank which had foreclosed on the building. We got that bank to finance the purchase for us 100% and finance the repair costs for us 100% so we basically bought a building with zero money down doing a construction project 100% financed by the selling bank.

Looking at every project creatively is one of the things to keep in mind when evaluating how to finance the deal. The worst they can do is say no. There are a lot of different ways you can get financing and/or assemble your stack of financing on larger real estate deals. This does get easier as you get experience and have more of a track record for the bank to see your success

The Most Unlikely Secret

One tip we wish we had known when first starting out is that when it comes to the world of real estate investing bigger is better. The bigger the property the bigger the loan. It's actually easier to finance a larger building than smaller deals. This due to several different reasons.

One, if you're looking at a traditional loan from a bank, with a larger project, the bank is going to look more at the property than at you. If you're taking over a six or eight-unit small building, they're going to evaluate you, your experience and your background. The bank assumes that the project will be self-managed. With a small project it is very easy to have one or two people move out, which would make a dramatic difference in the building's performance. Therefore, your personal skills at keeping a building rented, and re-renting when required, makes all the difference.

If you're looking at a 30 or a 40 or a hundred-unit building, then the evaluation will stay focused more on the building and the project and less on you personally. This means bigger buildings are actually easier to finance when you're asking the bank for a traditional loan.

Also, if you're doing untraditional lending; if you're using partners or private money or other investors, there's a cost to setting up partnerships and/or other legal organizations or entities. This legal work is going to cost you the same amount of money whether you have one partner, two partners, or 10 partners. Your cost of that setup is way more justifiable and way easier to support on a larger deal. When a partner is looking at the deal, they're going to be more intrigued by, "Hey, I'll be a part of this large deal," as opposed to, "Well, I'll be a part of this small deal."

So, when you're looking at financing deals a good tip is that bigger projects are actually easier to finance than smaller projects and it is easier to spread static costs across a larger deal than a smaller one.

This can be a little intimidating, especially to new investors. The best way to overcome this fear is to evaluate deals that you are think maybe a little bit out of your reach. Keep in mind that the bigger the deal the better for you, your partners, and the bank financing the deal. Sometimes it may be a little more comfortable to look at something smaller because it doesn't feel quite as risky. However, the real secret to getting your deals financed is 'go big'.

Tips for Successful Cash Management

Cash is King

If you run out of cash on a project, you are toast. You want to preserve your cash to make sure that you have cash reserves and cash on hand. Don't spend it all on the down payment. Once you run short on cash, your project is in trouble.

We have found that when you have cash in the bank you tend not to be as smart or creative with your money. Start by saying, "How can I do this deal with zero money down?" You may not actually be able to achieve that goal and may have to put some money down, but it does force you to think outside the box.

There was a time when we had money in the bank, so we were able to put 20% down. The trouble was that because we had the money, we didn't look at the deal creatively. After we closed, we kicked ourselves and said, "It would sure be nice to have a little bit more money in the bank account versus putting the full 20% down. We should have gotten creative." So, from that experience, we now try to evaluate every deal as if we had no money, as if we were just starting out and this was our first apartment deal.

We try to ensure that we are putting the least amount of cash into a deal up front because this gives us a cushion if additional money for repairs or other issues is needed to finish the project. Starting with the assumption we have no starting money is a good strategy to help ensure that we are creative on the frontend. Even if we end up putting in money, it helps keep our reserves high and prevents us from over-paying.

So, as you approach a purchase imagine that you had no money to put into the deal. Think more creatively about how you would finance the project.

Could you bring in a partner? Even with a partner, you could take a good-sized ownership stake for assembling the deal, doing the legwork and getting the project assembled. They have invested the cash and you are the managing partner, so you get a higher rate of return and your partner gets a chance to invest in real estate without having to do all the work.

You might be surprised at who would be interested in investing with you. Remember from our personal example, this could even be the bank. Think and evaluate creatively. This will help you grow faster and keep cash in your pocket for emergencies.

Ask for More

As long as you know the property can support it, ask for more than you think you need. The bank or your partner or whomever can always say no. This goes back to the fact that cash is king. Even if you don't think you will need it, this will give you a cushion which could be a lifesaver in the end if you have a bumpy road along the way. You do not want to run short on cash.

You only get one chance at the front end to build up all this financing. If you're six months or 12 months in and are running short on cash, you don't want to be going back to your partner or your lender or your bank, and saying, "Hey, I'm short on cash. We need some more money." Even if they are willing to lend it, which they may not be, the request is going to send your relationship with your lenders downhill fast. If they don't lend it things get even worse.

We saw a great example of this. We actually call it the 'Romeo spiral' because there was an apartment investor we knew whose name was Romeo and he ran out of cash for his apartments. Therefore, he started fixing plumbing issues with duct tape. He stopped fixing up the properties. If the roof had a leak, he wouldn't fix it because he didn't have the cash.

He was trying to get the cash by renting the units, but the only people who are going to live in a unit that has duct tape for plumbing and leaks in the roof are people who are transient and less likely to pay rent. Therefore, he was getting one month's rent when they moved in and then two or three months later they would stop paying. He would have to spend money to evict them or he wouldn't have the money to be able to evict them and he ended up letting them stay there for free.

This became a downward spiral because the less rent he was collecting from his tenants, the less money he had to fix up the units. The units got into worse condition. He had to rent to people willing to live in these worse conditions. They were less likely to pay rent, so he had less money to fix up the units.

It is definitely a spiral once you run out of money. You can get in trouble very, very quickly. Romeo ended up having to sell almost all of his buildings for extreme discounts because by the time he acknowledged his situation the apartments were extremely rundown. Instead of having just some minor fix-ups, all the units in the buildings required a gut rehab. There was water damage everywhere and the roofs were totally shot. He ended up having to sell the apartments for a substantial discount to even get out of them just because he had no cash to fix them.

We just recently heard that the buildings he couldn't sell he just walked away from and moved to another country. This is a very sad story which could have been avoided if he would have kept good cash reserves and had gotten the financing he really needed up front when he bought the buildings.

The Cash Trick Using Credits

There is a cool trick we have used several times when it comes to financing real estate deals. We get the seller to agree to provide us with credits and then finance those credits with the bank.

When you're purchasing a building, you will have a contract price but sometimes when you're doing your due diligence you might find, "Hey, there's a little more work needed here than I thought. Appliances are dated so there are probably going to be more things I'm going to need to replace." Rather than just asking for a discount on the purchase, ask for a seller credit. Not all institutions will finance on this, but quite a few will consider these credits as part of your input when you are closing on the property.

If your lender finances based on the full contract price but the seller is only receiving the price minus the credits, you are basically able borrow a little more to finance the construction of the repair costs.

This is not full-blown construction, but the extra repair costs you're going to be spending on the property. It's money you will be spending either way if you find the building needs some additional work, but this way the bank can help finance it up front. It's a great way to make sure you keep enough cash on hand.

For example, if you have a $100,000 deal and your lender will give you a loan on 80% then you will need to bring $20,000 to the close. If, during your inspection, you find the building needs an additional $10,000 of repairs you can ask for discount on the purchase price or you can ask for a credit.

If you ask for a discount on the purchase price, then the bank will only loan you 80% of the new purchase price of $90,000. So, you would need to bring $18,000 to the table for the down payment plus the $10,000 of repairs. This would mean a total of $28,000 to buy the building and complete the repairs.

If, on the other hand, you ask for a seller credit of $10,000 at the closing, then the bank will still lend on 80% of the purchase price of $100,000 because the official purchase price is still $100,000. In this scenario, you would need to bring only $10,000 to close because the other $10,000 is covered by the credit. In this case the all-in amount with purchase and repairs would be $20,000. As you deal with larger properties this math gets bigger.

I've found in most cases sellers are open to credits instead of money off the deal because to them it's really the same thing.

For example, let's say it's a million-dollar deal. You go through and you find there's a certain number of kitchens that have older appliances, a certain number of the furnaces are a little bit older than you thought so you realize, "There is maybe another 10,000 or $20,000 of work that I need to do."

From the seller standpoint, you're just asking for $20,000 off what they were going to get, whether it's structured as a credit or as a change in the price. It doesn't impact them directly because it doesn't alter the final amount they walk away with.

The impact is on your side and allows you to finance the construction instead of paying out of pocket after you have closed. You don't want to get into the building with a big down payment and then start burning through your cash as you need to do the extra work.
Make sure that during your due diligence you clearly document which things are different from what you expected. It should not be, "Oh, I just want a $50,000 credit because I want to pay less for the property." In theory, your offer and your agreed purchase price was based on your initial assumptions. Therefore, when you go back and ask for a credit, it should be based on finding things that were not what you thought they would be.

Before you have a building under contract you can only see the vacant units. Maybe you only saw one apartment that was brand new and everything was updated. The furnace was new. The kitchen was new. Everything was brand new.

Then, when the building is under contract you inspect all the occupied units and you find some of them have not been updated in 10 years. It's not the level of finish or condition that you initially thought.

If your offer was based on the one unit you viewed, you may have offered higher than you would have if you had known the full condition of all the apartments.

If there are differences such as in this case where the other units were older or in worse condition, then you have a legitimate reason to ask for credits. You were presented with the vacant unit and told that the whole building was in this condition. The reality, however, was that other units were older, dated, or whatever the differences might be.

This is where you get specific. You can say, "Hey, I want a concession because X number of kitchens were older than the unit we were initially shown. X number of furnaces were older than what we were initially shown." It's a legitimate tactic. You are really saying, "This building is not worth as much because of what we found."
The key to remember is that if it doesn't meet your expectations or assumptions, you have a legitimate case to go back and say, "Hey, because of this, this, and this we need a credit back." Then you can work with the bank to get financing on that credit, or have that credit used as your cash in the deal.

Taking this price reduction as a credit helps you finance those repairs that you know you're going to have to do.

When you're submitting your new proposal to the seller you should list out each item that the credit will be used for. You should also do this for the bank when you are asking them to finance the credit.

You want to be detailed because that will help put the bank at ease. You're not tricking anybody. It's just a way that you're financing a little bit more of your repair cost.

The seller is very clear on why you're asking for more off the cost. That's why they are likely to agree to it.

The bank also knows, "Hey, the buyer is getting this credit because of work that is needed," so they know the money is going back into building. They feel more comfortable because you are going to invest that money in the project.

The repairs will occur after close, and it may not be immediately. Just because it's an older kitchen doesn't mean that the stove will go out right away, but you do know it's going to go out sooner than the others. This way you will have the cash on hand to fix that stove when it does go out. In the meantime, you have some extra 'buffer' money in your account in case anything else major occurs with the property.

Knowing that these are legitimate expenses that will be going back into the building helps everyone understand and agree to what you are doing. That's why it's a legitimate way to finance additional work on your building.

The key is to keep in mind what your assumptions were during the evaluation and make sure that when you are in the building doing your due diligence anything that mismatches gets recorded.

This is a great way to finance. It is a nice little trick to get a bit more financing out of your project without over-leveraging.

A Cool True Story About Financing Deals Using a 10-31 Exchange

How a building is financed on the front end can really impact what you end up doing with a property down the road. This is a story of how we bought 28 units for 5% down and turned it into 76 units. This did take a few years to achieve, but it was a great project that helped to increase our growth.

The first building was a 28-unit foreclosure that was not performing well and was not in the best condition. We still assumed that everything was pretty consistent throughout the property.

When we did our due diligence and inspections of the building, we found some of the occupied units were in worse condition than what we thought. In addition, we found the plumbing required replacing and several of the furnaces had been damaged due to vandalism. During the initial review we didn't notice these issues.

The offer we put on the building was based on the assumptions we had made. Therefore, we went back to the seller, which happened to be a bank, and asked for a credit at close rather than a discount on the purchase price. We were using traditional bank financing on this deal, and the bank was willing to finance up to 85% of the purchase price. We had already sent them all of the information when we originally got the building under contract, including the contract price. They had approved the loan amount based on the contract price we provided them.

When we found out the building had more issues than we realized we asked for credits instead of money off the contract price. The bank giving us the loan agreed to finance against those credits. They had already agreed to the total amount of the loan, so they decided not to change the loan amount. Instead they reduced the amount of money that we needed to bring to the closing table.

Between the credits and the proration of rents (a benefit of closing on the 5th of the month) we effectively only had to bring 5.5% of the purchase price to close. This allowed us to keep our cash liquid. Especially since we knew the building needed a lot of work. We were able to go in, fix it up, increase the rents, and increase occupancy. We really stabilized the building. It turned into a great project with a strong cash-on-cash return.

[For those don't know a cash-on-cash return is the cash out of a deal vs. the cash you put into a deal. This is very similar to a return on investment (ROI) but you are purely measuring cash. This is critical to look at for investments to see how quickly you are getting the cash you invested into a deal back out into your pocket.]

The downside of this deal was that it was in a less stable area that was far away from our other buildings. This made it very tough for our maintenance team and property management to get back and forth effectively. Therefore, we decided to sell it after we had fixed it up.

We had increased occupancy and the rents had significantly climbed, so we knew we could get our money back out again. We were able to get it under contract fairly quickly and when we sold the building, we did a 10-31 exchange.

A 10-31 exchange is when you take the capital gains proceeds from one building and roll it into another building as a down payment. This is currently available on like-for-like properties. This allows you to defer any capital gains taxes you would have had to pay by rolling those proceeds over into a new building. It's a tax delay, and useful if you want to keep all of your proceeds and know you are going to continue to invest. We would recommend talking to your accountant if you think you may qualify for this program.

One nice feature of this program is that you can roll your proceeds from one property into multiple properties. We sold this 28 unit. We had already identified a couple of buildings we were looking to purchase.

We were able to use that money as a down payment from the exchange to buy a 40 unit. We were able to finance the 40 unit for around 90% of its contract price so we had extra cash left over in the 10-31 exchange account.

Therefore, we did a second project with the rest of the proceeds that bought us a 24 unit and a 12 unit. For these properties we brought a partner in to make up the difference in our remaining funds and the required down payment, which was around 19% of the overall deal for the 24 and 12-unit deals.

We used the advantage of the exchange, used the advantage of partners, and used the advantage of credits to roll one 28-unit building into three buildings totaling 76 units and didn't pay any capital gains taxes along the way.

This is a pretty good example of how you can get creative with both your acquisition and exit strategy to really grow your business.

Financing has a huge impact on your bottom line. This is where creativity can really accelerate your growth and maximize your return.

A Big Opportunity with Real Estate

A huge opportunity that people sometimes forget is working with local banks. Many local banks hold loans "in house." They are called a portfolio loan, so they are not making the loan to you and then selling it off to somebody else.

They're keeping this inside their bank or "in house." This is part of their investment strategy, so they're investing in you and in the project. The interest you pay them is going back into their bank. Because of this they're able to be a bit more creative and flexible. In addition, if they are local, they usually also understand local areas. They understand certain markets. They will be able to help you understand which projects make sense, and what certain areas are looking like.

They can become an excellent partner and resource. You can build a relationship with a local bank and get feedback on some of your plans. This can be really hard to do with a large, national bank.

There are of course additional ways to finance including partners and other various options, however, working with local banks is a really good opportunity.

When financing is competitive, there are a lot of banks trying to finance large real estate deals. They want to grow their lending pool in that investment class so they're getting very competitive.

With this situation, sometimes there are local banks that actually have significantly better terms than national banks. Their committee that's approving the loans is local, so it generally should be a faster approval process.

Faster approval is better because you don't want to find out your financing fell through as you are coming up to the closing.

You want to be sure you're working with somebody that you trust, that you know can close and that trusts you and your project. There is a great opportunity to build this type of relationship when working with local banks.

Don't, however, just stick with one bank. You need to build multiple relationships. Sometimes, especially if they are smaller banks, they may reach a limit of how much they can lend to one individual. There are various federal regulations that cap their limit of exposure to a single investor.

Make sure you cultivate relationships with multiple local lenders, local bankers that are doing commercial lending, not residential lending, but the ones that are doing commercial real estate lending.

Some of the Biggest Challenges with Real Estate

One of the challenges is when there is a large interest in apartment investing. There are loads of investors looking and there are many banks that want to lend. There are not a ton of deals available. The challenge then is getting the deals to close.

The trade-off is that you have more options to find the right deal. With more buyers, prices are usually up, and current owners are more willing to sell.

To make all this work, however, it helps if you know the ability of your bank, partner(s), and/or your lender to perform. There are several things you can do to give yourself some security around this.

If you are using one or more partners, make sure they move their committed money into an escrow account long before the closing. That way you know the funds are truly available and your partner is committed, at least to the level of putting their money into an escrow account.

It doesn't mean you have to have access to that account, but it does show they have the money and are basically committed. You don't want to find out at the last minute, "Oh, they're not actually committed or they're not financially able to pull it off at the dollar level they implied."

In addition, you need to get a commitment from them to make sure they're not only committed to general investing but investing in a specific project. We had a partner that kept sitting on the fence. They were non-committal on whether they were in or out on this one particular project. Then they suddenly became very difficult to reach as we were coming up on our close date. Luckily, we had another option for that project.

Make sure you have a backup resource for those funds. That way you can show them, "Hey, we moved forward. We closed with another partner. We closed with this other financing.
This was an opportunity you missed out on. Going forward, you need to let us know if you are in or out, or you're going to keep missing out on these opportunities." By having back-up plans you can build a track record to say, "Hey, you have to commit, or you miss out."

So, with individual partners or any non-bank financing, you need to make sure as early as possible that they are committed and have set aside the funds. If they haven't made the commitment and put up the funds, then you need options and a backup plan, so you can close on the project.

The last thing you want to do is arrive at the closing without the funds. You could actually end up in a lawsuit for failure to perform, and that's not where anybody wants to be.

Another example of a challenge we've had with financing was when we were using a traditional bank. The bank became nervous with the low amount of cash that we wanted to bring to close, due to some of our other creative activities such as credits. They were financing the deal and the bank wanted us to have more of our own money invested in the deal.

In this example the bank was not satisfied with the amount we were putting down, but instead of just accepting the bank saying, "We need you to put more money down," we were creative. We asked the bank for options.

Remember this is a business. This is a negotiation with whoever is doing your financing whether this is a bank, a partner, a hard money lender, or whatever other entity. Don't necessarily take the first offer. The bank would have loved for us just to put more money into the building, but we were able to negotiate with the bank and instead put a certain amount of cash into an escrow account.

We were allowed to draw on the funds to help fix up the property. This allowed us to make sure that we had the cash that was needed to fix up the property and not necessarily just hand it over to the bank at the beginning as part of our 20%.

This is another advantage of working with local banks. These things are much easier to negotiate because their local approval committee is nearby. They can discuss your proposed options.

Ultimately, what everybody – banks, lenders and partners, are looking for is some level of security. If you're going into a deal with no money down, because you have financed the whole thing or partners are bringing in all the money, your financers may be somewhat concerned and say, "Well, you don't have any risk in this project because you don't have any money in your name."

Sometimes you can get around that with exactly the scenario we just mentioned where, "Well, we're going to put some money in escrow," so the bank has a collateral pledge of, "Okay. If everything goes wrong, I know I can take the money out of this account, but if everything goes fine, we'll release that money back to you."

Rather than putting the money in now, doing the project, and then pulling the money back out through a cash-out refi, you basically are pre-paying for that refinance and setting the money aside. You are saying, "Okay. If the project does X, Y, and Z, you'll release those funds back to me." Then you don't have to pay for a refinance. You don't have to pay for a new loan, but you can get your money back out of the project and the bank is still satisfied because now the project is done. Now the property has the cash flow that it needs.

Situations like this are typically only going to be seen when you are doing a renovation or some sort of change to the building. When that is the case they might say, "We'll only need that collateral pledge for a certain period of time until we can see that the building is actually performing the way we expect it to." Once you have a track record where the building has cash flow and it has been paying all the debt for 12 months, generally the banks will be very comfortable with that finance level.

That extra cash at the frontend in an escrow account is a great way to put a bank at ease, get a little more creative with your leverage, and get your cash back out once the project or the renovations are done.

The Trick to Using Resources

If you are interested in using partners or exchanges, there are some resources that you need to work with to help you understand your options and how they impact your business.

Anytime you're dealing with any sort of tax-related plan, such as a 10-31 exchange, you will need to consult with your accountant.

Note that when we say accountant, we don't mean H&R Block. You need to have a real estate or business accountant. Someone who deals with property owners and know the laws and regulations. Your accountant will be the person to advise you regarding the tax implications.

For example, on the 10-31 exchange it only defers your taxes, it doesn't stop them. So, you would need to work with your accountant to determine if you're in a position to pay your taxes now or if waiting would be better. They would also help with the logistics of using the tax shelters. In the previous example we had to put the funds into an escrow account directly from the sale. We couldn't touch any of the money, or the whole thing would be voided. Your accountant will help ensure that you are following all of the proper guidelines so that you don't accidentally miss an opportunity.

Also, you will need to make sure you have a real estate attorney on your team. When it comes to partnerships, the sky is the limit. There's a lot of different ways you can partner with people. Again, a real estate attorney or some sort of attorney that does real estate transactions and real estate partnerships is a great resource to just talk about ideas based on how they have seen other people structure deals.

They might not be able to give you specifics on who's involved because of confidentiality, but they can certainly say, "Hey, we've structured deals like this. We've arranged partnerships. We've had multiple partners. We've had general partners and ones with a silent partner or a managing partner and a financial partner." They're a good resource to use to get ideas on what you can do.

Really, with all these processes you need a team of resources. Some people may not like the idea of paying an accountant or a lawyer, especially one that specializes in real estate. They feel that with enough research they can handle all these decisions on their own.

We would caution against the approach of self-representation. With all the changes to the tax law and the litigious state of our country these resources can and will save you a lot more money than they cost. Plus, having professionals on your side will also help banks, partners, and future partners feel more at ease dealing with you. You will come across as professional, and if any of them have a question you can't answer directing them to your accountant is a lot better than telling them you need to look it up on google. These resources are worth the cost and should be part of your team.

Also, we have known situations where people, for whatever the reason, have tried to have partnerships without setting up an official partnership agreement. Technically, anytime two people put money together and purchase something, that is a partnership. That is an agreement. If it's a marriage, if it's a car, if it's a house, if it's an apartment building, anytime two people come together that is a partnership.

You don't necessarily need to have a partner's agreement to have a partnership, but it is highly recommended. As long as everything is working well, there's no need for a partnership agreement. The reason you put one into place is if something goes wrong. The prenuptial agreement is only used during the break-up, much like partnership agreements are more about what happens when things stop working well.

If you've purchased a building and it needs more money, where does that money come from? Who puts that money in? Who gets paid back first? If you need to sell, if there's a divorce in the family or a death in the family and one of the partners needs money, do you have first right of purchase? Can they force a sale? These are the types of things that can be found in partnership agreements, which is why it is so important that you properly structure the partnership deal.

It is very highly recommended to make sure that a proper real estate attorney who's used to dealing with the property types that you are looking at and the sizes you are looking at is engaged with everything you're doing. Don't go to a divorce attorney and ask them to put together partnership documentation for a partnership on a multimillion-dollar apartment deal.

Make sure that the people you have on the team are the right people for the job. We actually have multiple lawyers on our team. One lawyer specializes in evictions.

One lawyer specializes in partnerships and deals. One lawyer focuses on estate planning and financial structures. So, we have three lawyers on our team that we know we can contact based on what we need from them.

It's very important not just to say, "Oh, I have a lawyer on my team," but you must be sure you have the right lawyers for the projects that you're working on. This is also true for accountants. Make sure you have an accountant that understands business and real estate. Lawyers and accounts are great resources to have on your side.

Apartment investing is a very small world compared to single-family investing or even small duplex-type style investing. There are not that many people comparatively that do it, so if you're talking to an accountant who has experience with apartments and real estate investing, he probably knows other people that do apartments and real estate investing.

This might be a great opportunity to get contacts or partners or find out when people are selling. Accountants know early on if someone's going to be selling or dealing with a death or a divorce or anything that will mean changing their tax structure. Accountants are going to know what is happening with other people in their circle, so having an accountant you know, and trust can be a huge asset.

The same is true with attorneys. If someone is being sued or someone is taking people to court, they will know what is happening. Not just on the negative side but, also, on the positive. They know other people that are investing. If you build a relationship, they might be able to help with introductions. You could find deals, partners, or just build your local network of investors.

These resources will benefit you in multiple ways, so it is very important that you make these connections and have a solid team when investing in larger real estate deals.

Time Management Tips in a Busy Real Estate World

The Right Things Up Front Can Save Time in the End

We are all busy people. We have families, jobs, obligations. Managing our time is very important to everyone, but especially new real estate investors. A good way to save time and heartburn when financing deals is to make sure that you have multiple options to close. Especially with 'risky' financing.

If you are partnering with someone for the first time and you don't know a lot about them, you may want to make sure that you are covered in case they fail to perform. We had one deal where we thought we had an investor but when his spouse heard about it, the whole thing was off. Luckily, we had a back-up plan.

At the beginning of a project make sure to call multiple banks to get competitive quotes. This is true even if in the past you have used the same bank. You never know when the bank will change their policies, or lending requirements.

If you're talking to partners, talk to multiple partners. Make sure you have options. You don't want to be stuck approaching the deadline of a closing and not able to perform because of your lending.

Also, you don't want to waste a lot of your time pursuing one partner or counting on one bank only to find out that your project isn't the right one for them. Getting yourself in that situation could lead to multiple issues from loss of trust with your broker that you can't close all the way up to being sued for failure to perform at close. It is very important to make sure that you have everything you need lined up well before that closing date, just in case something goes wrong.

In addition, it is critical that you are constantly in contact with multiple financing opportunities like banks, potential partners, or alternative lending institutions. Make sure you have your options open, make sure you know enough of the current market to know good terms. If you're dealing with banks, multiple banks will give you better terms. Multiple partners will give you security of knowing, "Hey, if this guy can't pull it off this time, someone else can." That it is important, to make sure you don't waste your time and that you're successful, you must have multiple groups or investment options every time you're looking at a deal.

Another tip for time management is to be sure that you have all the documentation you need up front. Generally, you only have about 15, maybe 30 days, on your due diligence. That is when you're doing your evaluation of the building, and really looking at the project.
Maybe it's 30 to 45 days on your financing timeline so after you pass 45 days if you haven't said, "No. I don't have the financing for it," you're obligated. Your escrow money, or your earnest money that you've put down is now at risk. The seller can take that and if you are not able to close after you have passed all of your contingencies, they can sue you for breach of contract.

You only have a month, a month and a half, two months at the most to know if your financing is in place and still get out of the deal if it looks like it's falling apart. After you pass that window, your money is committed. The seller gets to take any earnest money you put down.

Again, if you fail to perform, you're subject to breach of contract. I've actually had to threaten a purchaser with a lawsuit. We were selling a property and for whatever the reason, the buyer got confused on the transaction and did not want to sign the closing documents.

Basically, she would have been in breach of contract and that would have involved a lawsuit where she would have been liable for damages and whatever else might have come up.
There is always a risk with real estate investing. Just make sure you have everything lined up in advance including your documentation and knowing how you will structure your partnership and/or other financial arrangements.

This means, when you're doing that evaluation look at how your finance piece is stacking up, how much money you're bring in yourself, how much is coming from partners and how much is coming from a bank. Make sure you have each one of those identified and committed before that finance contingent time runs out so you know you can bring everything to the closing.

Avoid This Time-Wasting Trap

People waste a lot of time talking to people who don't finance deals. Again, we're talking about creativity in the real estate world. You may be used to financing small, single-family homes or your own personal residence, but if you talk to that same bank or lender or institution many of them won't understand apartment financing and probably won't be able to actually finance your deal. They won't be able to get it through their approval process to close. Therefore, make sure the person you're talking to either as a partner or a lender has been involved in large real estate transactions in the past.

If you talk to the correct people, you'll be able to get your financing lined up fairly quickly. Don't waste time talking to people who may want to help you out but won't be able to because they don't have the experience or track record. It will save time and you are more likely to succeed if you talk with people who have past experience financing large real estate deals.

The Trick to knowing the Current Financing Situation and Taking Advantage

The real estate market is very cyclical. The market from 2006 was different than 2009 and is very different from 2017. As apartment markets heat up, there are some things that make it easier for investors.

There are a lot more lenders financing projects, especially traditional lenders like banks. When we started on our first deal in the 2009 down market, we went through 27 banks before we found a bank that would finance the property for us. In an up market, there are a lot more banks that are interested in financing commercial real estate deals.

In an up market, Banks are more competitive with financing so that's to your advantage. When you're trying to finance a deal, there will be more banks trying to compete for it. You're going to get better terms and better options on your financing.

There is a challenge that some banks that want to invest in larger real estate deals don't have very much experience in that area of lending. Maybe it has been a while since they lent on a larger real estate deal, or maybe they're trying to grow into a new area or bigger deals. You want to make sure they have a good track record for what you want to do.

I've encountered a few banks that said, "Yeah. We're growing on the apartment side. We really want to finance new deals," so you send them deals and they debate and are not aggressive about it. You need to quickly identify that, "This is not really someone who's going to commit and follow through." You should focus on the banks and investors that have done this before or have a decent track record so that you know they can perform.

The last thing you want to happen is to get to close and not have your financing ready. Make sure you have everything lined up. The good news is there are more banks out there. Watch out for the ones that haven't done this before are trying to get into this type of investing. They might be a little too cautious and nervous on your deal.

Even if a lender is experienced but especially if they are not, make sure you have multiple options. That way if they fall through, you have somebody else already lined up.

Final Thoughts on Financing

As we mentioned, and counter to intuitive thought, the bigger deals are actually easier to finance. It doesn't have to be a $10 million deal to be a bigger deal, but an easy rule of thumb is that a million-dollar deal is a lot easier to finance than $100,000 deal. At a million dollars, some of the costs for setting up partnerships are lower and it adds appeal as a place for people to invest.

Also, looking at the dollar return, if you get a 10 or 15% return on a million-dollar deal, that's $100,000-$150,000. That's worth doing some partnerships. If you get that same 15% return on a $100,000 deal, that's $15,000. You may write a check to an attorney for five-grand to get everything set up for you so that burns through profit margin pretty quickly.

The larger deals, the ones where you can afford to bring on multiple people may give you a better dollar return even if it is a lower percentage rate. Look at smaller deals very carefully, even if you get a higher return rate, because they still might not be the best deal to try to pursue. They might actually be very tough for someone to finance for you. If you're looking for partners, if you're looking for financing, those larger deals are more appealing to more partners and to more banks.

However, whatever size project you decide to pursue, make sure you have those multiple financing options lined up to help guarantee you can make it to the closing table.

In conclusion, apartment investing may sound challenging, but it does get easier with experience and with a track record to show your skills. It just takes getting started and intending to succeed.

Be prepared, be creative and be persistent.

We hope, now that you have read this section, you have a much clearer understanding of how to finance your buildings which should take you a long way toward successful apartment investing.

Have a great day.

CLOSING

We have enjoyed sharing our thoughts and experiences related to finding and financing your apartment buildings. We hope our information will help you move toward a successful apartment investing career.

To take the next step, you may want to read our other book: _Managing Apartments for Profit – Tips and Tricks for Taking Over and Managing Apartments_ which is available at Amazon.